RAW

life or death --

the setting is now
it is sept —
it is fall —
a woman sitting on the
stairs peeling an apple in
one piece staring at her lover
a young blonde girl
digging a hole with a spoon
her mother taking it from
her — angry
a boy and girl pushing
closer in the bushes
hiding —
grandma ... is
a blue
(or a
endless
those and
bell — ... has
been kn... for 100
years ...)

a teenage ... freckles
blowing
pink bubble...

lets her ...
gently ...
— she
him tak...
bound tied...
on from
passion...
icy de...
the sh...
in part...
fill ma...
es —
ts —
challe...
happ...
some...
over...
with

RAW

PAMELA ANDERSON
AND EMMA DUNLAVEY

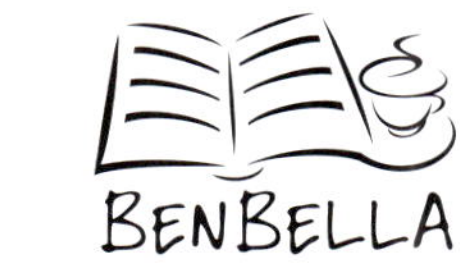

BenBella Books, Inc.

Dallas, Texas

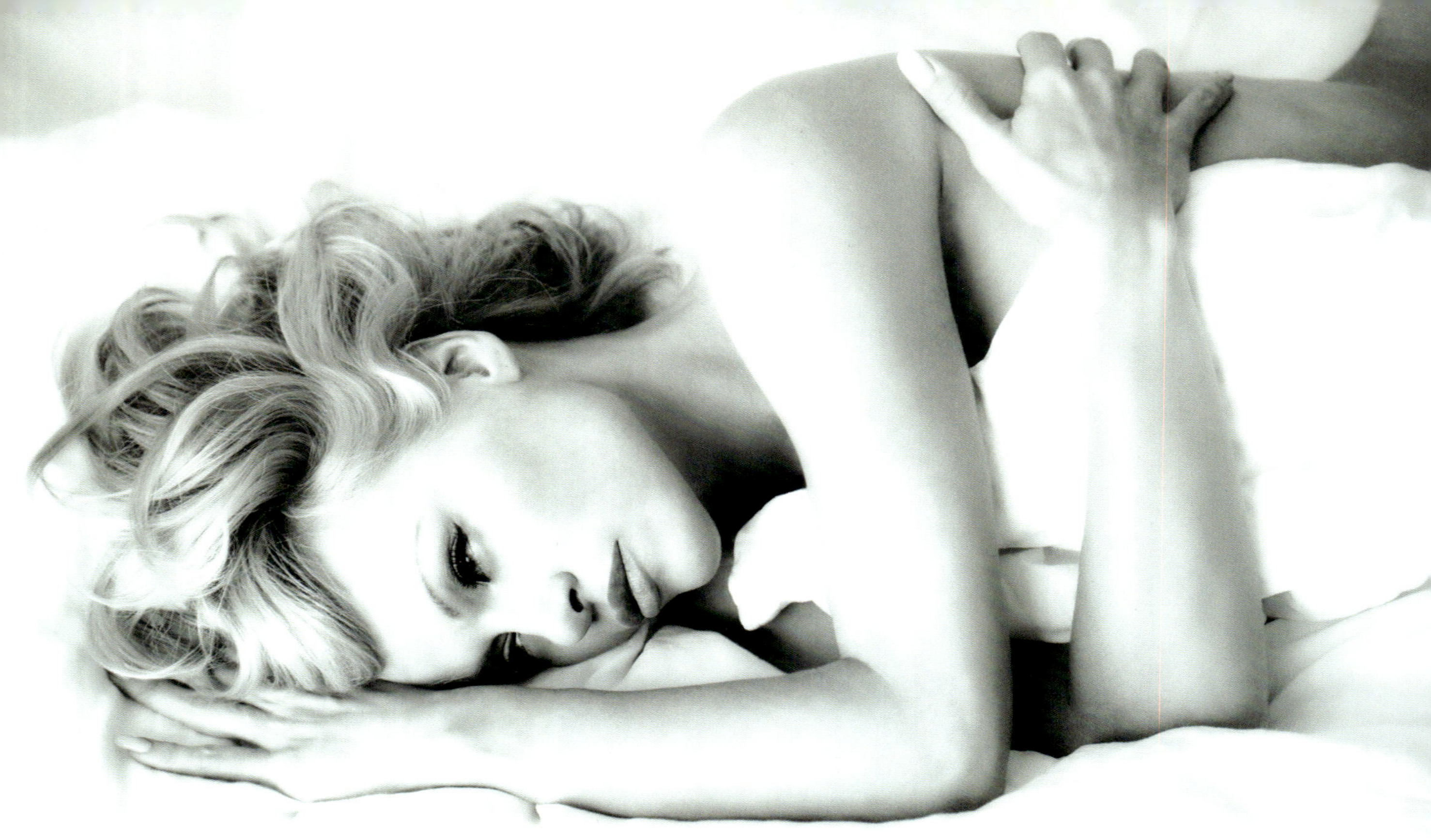

imaginary lovers
&
make believe
friends

FOREWORD

Sometimes the world brings beautiful people into it. With Pam, it brought beauty on the inside and out! A beautiful soul with an amazing mind. She has the depth, mystery, beauty and everything one truly desires. On every organic level. The ability to be completely raw.

Emma's photographs give you a serene feeling to rise above the many challenges we face in the world today. Your thoughts become only about love and *true* love. Her effortless visual ability allows the reader to dream and only want to feel the beauty.

The two animals are a match made in heaven.

The perfect word to describe Pam for me would be pure *passion*, in both the heart and soul of our existence. Something that could never be forced–it comes from a very sacred place hidden in her heart.

The essence of these photographs portray that hidden wisdom, almost in a surreal way, thinking about the moment. Where Pam and Emma were when they truly captured that moment does not matter.

A moment in one's mind will always be the way with Pam–people cannot forget.

Beauty is integrated with nature–the most spiritual quality I believe, and it does not matter where this was photographed.

Emma's true reality has never left her English countryside, horses, harmony with nature, and raw passion. This life is meant for beautiful collaborations. To make the world a better place, to grow and learn like aboriginals always believed.

To return home, to the earth, and the universe.

In every moment in time something beautiful can happen, and when true artists like Emma and Pamela integrate, the magic blossoms and fills with organic sensibilities.

Pamela makes me dream and see everything in such a unique way.

She makes you let go.

She makes you want to let go.

She makes you want to feel.

You are left only with true love and beauty; it's her secret, and not a dark one.

Open like a book, and this is why these photographs compliment her so much.

Bob Marley once said: "Some people feel the rain. Others just get wet."

These girls feel the rain *and* get wet!

–RAPHAEL MAZZUCCO

INTRODUCTION

I live beneath the
    lowest breath-past
    indecision . . .
I have Faith,
I'm painting a picture-
A sculpture in lights . . .

There is an energy in me-
healthy, wild, and
    stirring . . .

A "Somnambulist"-living in
    a consistent dream state-

Ecstasy,
Blissful, and challenging-
it comes with a price . . .
I draw people to me-who are
difficult-
and when you peel back
the layers-left vulnerable-
wide open-it's a dangerous
    playground-
but, a lovely one-
loving relentlessly from the
    deepest parts-
having the strength to pull
    back-dip in and out . . .
Intuitively knowing the

Volcano will erupt-to
    stand back.
Observe . . .
Love from a distance-

I'm a red hot poker-
Ask my kids-
I push it-
I hope to inspire loved ones
    to live with passion
to go to places no one else
    has-
We all have secrets
    inside . . .
(that drive us . . .)-
We all have a purpose-
It's curious to me-
Who are we? Why are we here?
It's not to just exist
    and take-
We are here to live . . .
and give-and be
    creative . . .

I don't know how I feel about
    beauty-
Or who decided what beauty is-
My mom says beauty comes
    from the inside-

it's ageless.
A lot burns inside this
    body . . .
A mischievous longing . . .
    cravings . . .
a wicked hunger-
I am an insatiable
    beast . . .

I believe we are all born
    with a plan . . .
I love who my boys are-
I also know . . . the
    dance . . .
When I want to give them
the world-
I must give them love
    instead-
They know every action has a
    repercussion-
good or bad-it's their
    choice.
I am grateful to have such
    interesting, bold, and
    brave boys.

Everyone deserves
    love . . . (especially
    those who don't believe
    they do)
I end up
biting off a lot . . .

I take big risks-

The most valuable currency I
    have is my heart.
I deserve to have loving,
    romantic relationships,
full of passion and
    kindness-but . . .
    with a twist . . .
    a challenge . . .
An unexpected feeling-
    abandonment of self-
to enter another's world.
Try it on . . . shape shift-

It's hard to believe that
    Emma and I have known
    each other over twenty
    years . . .
We have traveled the world
    together. She knows me so
    well . . . The good, bad
    and . . . ugly.
We've gotten ourselves
    into some pretty strange
    places-
And . . .
After all this time in
    each other's faces-
    we've become like
    sisters . . . I can't
    hide from her-it's a

relationship like no
other.
Makeup artists become
    confidants . . . they know
    all our secrets-
We both have a silly sense of
    humor-
and both feel deeply and
    care about the world-

Emma is a naturally talented
    photographer-
If I were shooting me-I'd
    be her.
We envision the same angles.
Being In the moment,
    present-within a
    fantasy . . .
We shoot quick and
    spontaneously. Like two
    little girls-
We are always laughing.

Luckily, even before she
    branched out and made
    this her profession-she
    always had her camera in
    her hand,
and we have record of some of
    our salacious adventures-
I appreciate that she's
    never tried to change me-

only encouraged me to
    be me-
It's organic-
I find it funny when
    people use the word
    "re-invention"-
Short hair doesn't make me a
    better actress . . .
and less eyeliner doesn't
    make
me a better wife . . .
(I tried . . . HA)

Watch out . . .
Tell someone what not to do-
and guess what happens. . . ?
The rebel is born.

Emma and I feel the same
    about celebrating sexy.
I've had an interesting and
    wild career so far-
And ACT II is getting even
    more bizarre-

I have learned to balance
    my life-
maybe compartmentalized
    a bit-
Nothing calculated.
It's actually quite
    innocent . . .

it's real.
This is my life-
I'm proud that I've been
    able to
bring meaning to it-
by using the attention
    to help-
The Pamela
    Anderson Foundation is
    my legacy-improving the
    lives of animals,
the environment, vulnerable
    people . . .
(including activists).
We support those on the
front lines-the freedom
    fighters . . . Artists.

I dare to LIVE . . . within a
    bohemian style freedom-to
embrace sexuality . . .
Repression is what gets us
    into trouble-
If we can respect each
    other-and respect
    ourselves-
There are no rules-
All my shenanigans are
    my own-
I'm actually an instigator-

What is my purpose?-

I think I found it-
it's to enjoy my life-
and make here and now a
    better place-
empower women to be all that
    they are-
And not let desensitization
    ruin the fun . . .
Being creative within
    healthy boundaries-
That's where Art is born-

I am sharing some of my most
    intimate and ridiculous
    moments-through poetry,
    journals, and Emma's fly-
    on-the-wall, ninja-style
    photography-(in knee
    pads) This is me RAW-This
    is a peek into my slightly
    naughty world-
I can't help but feel-
A constant inner giggle . . .

Love,

PAMELA X

...times If I
think
that water equals
an affair
should be
... of grief
... of
... waves.
... and
unpredictable
life never shows
us the end.
If the end is guaranteed
I know
Its my head stuck
in a cord keep
kicking for my
wife
without mercy

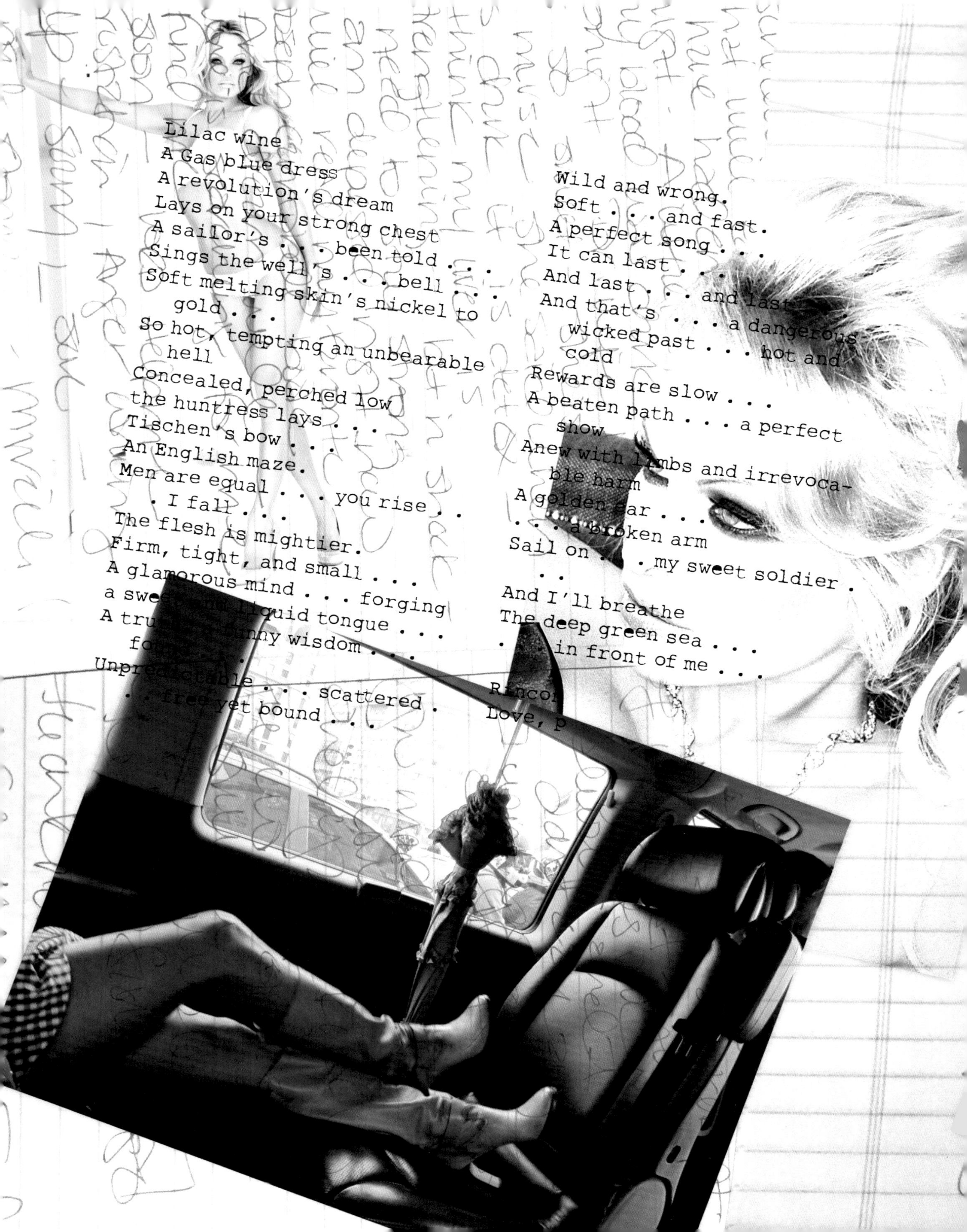

Lilac wine
A Gas blue dress
A revolution's dream
Lays on your strong chest
A sailor's . . . been told . . .
Sings the well's . . . bell . . .
Soft melting skin's nickel to
    gold . . .
So hot, tempting an unbearable
    hell
Concealed, perched low
the huntress lays . . . .
Tischen's bow . . . .
An English maze.
Men are equal . . . you rise
. . I fall
The flesh is mightier.
Firm, tight, and small
A glamorous mind . . . forging
a sweet and liquid tongue . . .
A trusting funny wisdom . . .
    fou . . . .
Unpredictable . . . scattered .
. . . free yet bound . . .

Wild and wrong.
Soft . . . and fast.
A perfect song . . .
It can last . . .
And last . . . and last
And that's . . . a dangerous
    wicked past . . . hot and
    cold
Rewards are slow . . .
A beaten path . . . a perfect
    show
Anew with lambs and irrevoca-
    ble harm
A golden ear . . .
. . . a broken arm
Sail on . . .
. . . my sweet soldier .
And I'll breathe
The deep green sea . . .
. . in front of me . . .
Rincon
Love, P

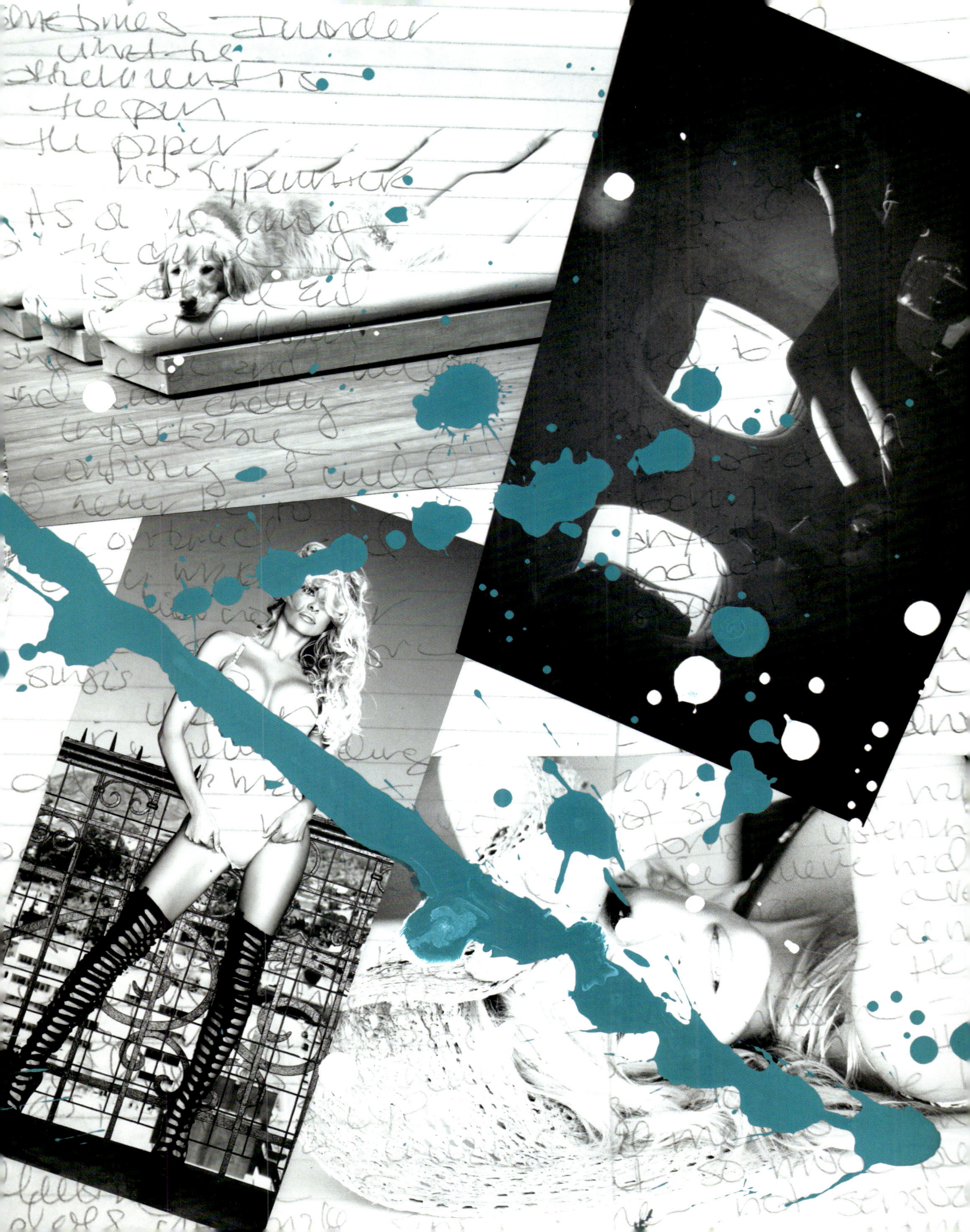

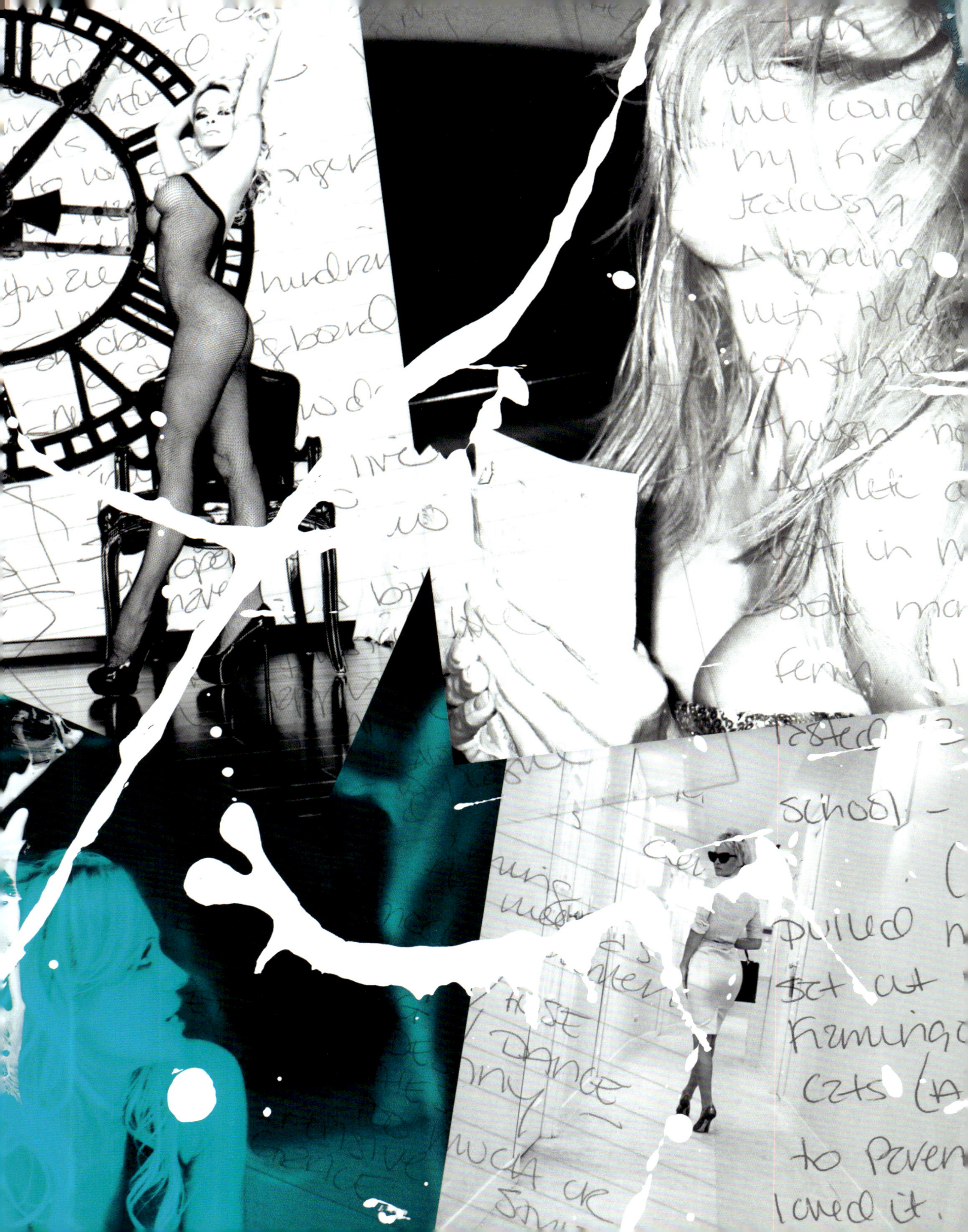

Sometimes I wish I were [illegible]

[illegible] me [illegible]

[illegible] developed — tiny [illegible]
[illegible] year, [illegible]
[illegible] Dad [illegible] me to [illegible]
[illegible] home [illegible]
[illegible] an apartment. [illegible]
[illegible] paid ½ of my [illegible]
1st Design job — [illegible]
[illegible] with [illegible]

the dream . . .
arousing my tenderness,
A sweet rawness-
feeling bruised and scratched
   up-
Hypnotic-
Life is sensual-not a "fix it
   in post"-
ME-I miss PLAYBOY-
The End of an Era-
Chivalry, elegance-
Celebrated imperfections-
differences . . . hot-passionate
   dreamy scenes . . .
The girl next door-shyness-
   "it's my first time"
but-not my last . . . (wink)
-I'm planning a mysterious
   coup-
Want to get in on it-
Julian Assange?
Is it healthy, to be fantasied
   about . . .
by many men-
Isn't that the goal-
How many can we affect-
It's natural-to want to be
   desired-
The world creeps up on you-
and there you are-
ALL over the place-
places you never intended to
   be- (desert storm?)
(soldiers)
I am human you know-
left to adjust to the madness-
No mercy-pay the price-my
   fault-

BG-feeling empty, sad-
   withdrawn-
Left to Isolate-Medicate.
Go to sleep-
ME-NO! I won't-
ME-You know-It's not freaky
   enough,
to just be beautiful-
I've never felt beautiful-
I always felt sexual . . . and
   blind . . .
oh wowwy . . . I'm losing my
   mind-
I'm shutting down-It's such a
   strange feeling . . .
going numb . . . in front of
   everyone-
It's like a Self-inflicted
   drowning . . . hard to do-
(Alarm bells!!)-
When did I want to be this
   thing?-
To attract what?
When did I go from a curious
   little girl,
to an insatiable woman? Girl on
   the run . . .
Femme fatale . . . devoted
   and . . . divided-
Are we all going crazy? -
or, is it just me?
Is it that stuff on unwashed
   vegetables?
When did I lose control over my
   own heart?-
When did I start believing,

magic hour . . .
ME-"Everyone looks good this
   early"
BG-Even cats and hummingbirds
Was anyone watching her . . .
She gazed up into dark
   windows . . .
to nobody . . .
and let the jacket fall loosely
   around
her shoulders . . .
The rush coming back . . .
a little lost on purpose,
Hiding around corners,
ME-"Dangerous-
my body is on fire . . .
my body is never done-trouble
   finds me-
please find me-
The iron is always hot!"
BG-She leaned against the cool
   wall of a
stony church-
It felt good, soothing-
ME-I wonder how prostitution
   works-
Does it ever feel good?
Lost little souls-being taken
   advantage of-
   taking advantage of-
Is it just for money? Is it for
   attention?
or-both-
Women suffer-
Everywhere-
rules, rules, rules
conflicting needs . . .

I can't find the answers-it's
   an epidemic-
I know I won't compete with a
   computer-
or-a gaggle of Hollywood boys
   hiring poor
Russian girls to swallow
   loaves of bread
up their anus?
or worse-sleep with fat hairy
   people?
How does that work?"
BG-She was disturbed-
How far can she take this?-Is
   it even real?
ME-"Have we lost men to thin
   air-
to the Abyss-
Flesh is attached to a heart and
   a brain
takes effort . . . and
   skill . . .
Where are the great lovers
   lost art . . .
God, I hope not . . .
I've never been to Columb[ia]
   Should I go?"
     Hysteria? . . .
     mortified . . .
now-Coming down the
   ceil[ing]
dripping . . .
dancing with . . .
   closed-
the dream . . .
arousing my tenderness

to rooms - it's never been
sex is returd - i've never had doors
when you are alone you are

something to be ashamed of
pruning back to blossom again...
cleaning house
cleaning your soul

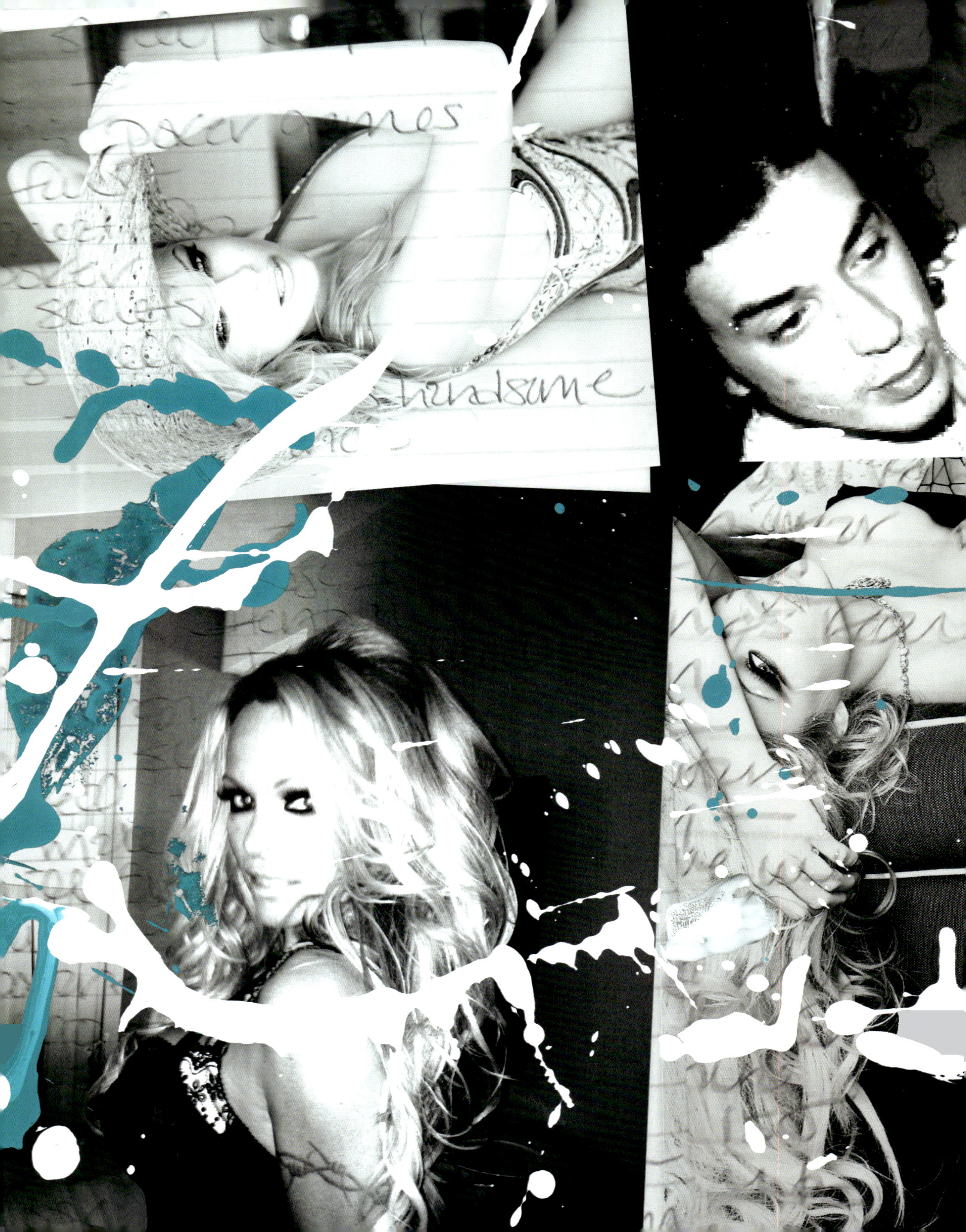

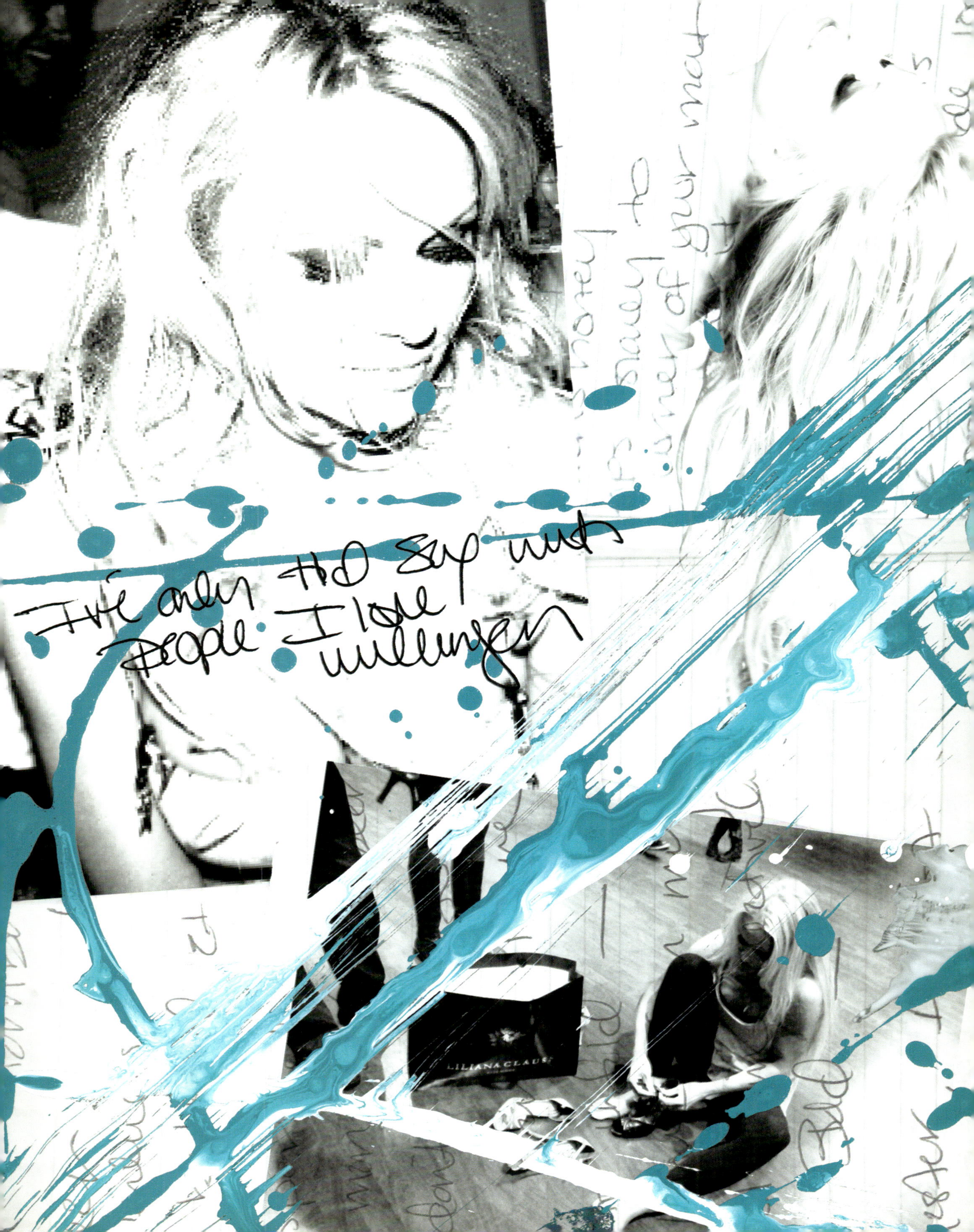

I've only had sex with
People I love
LILIANA CLAUS

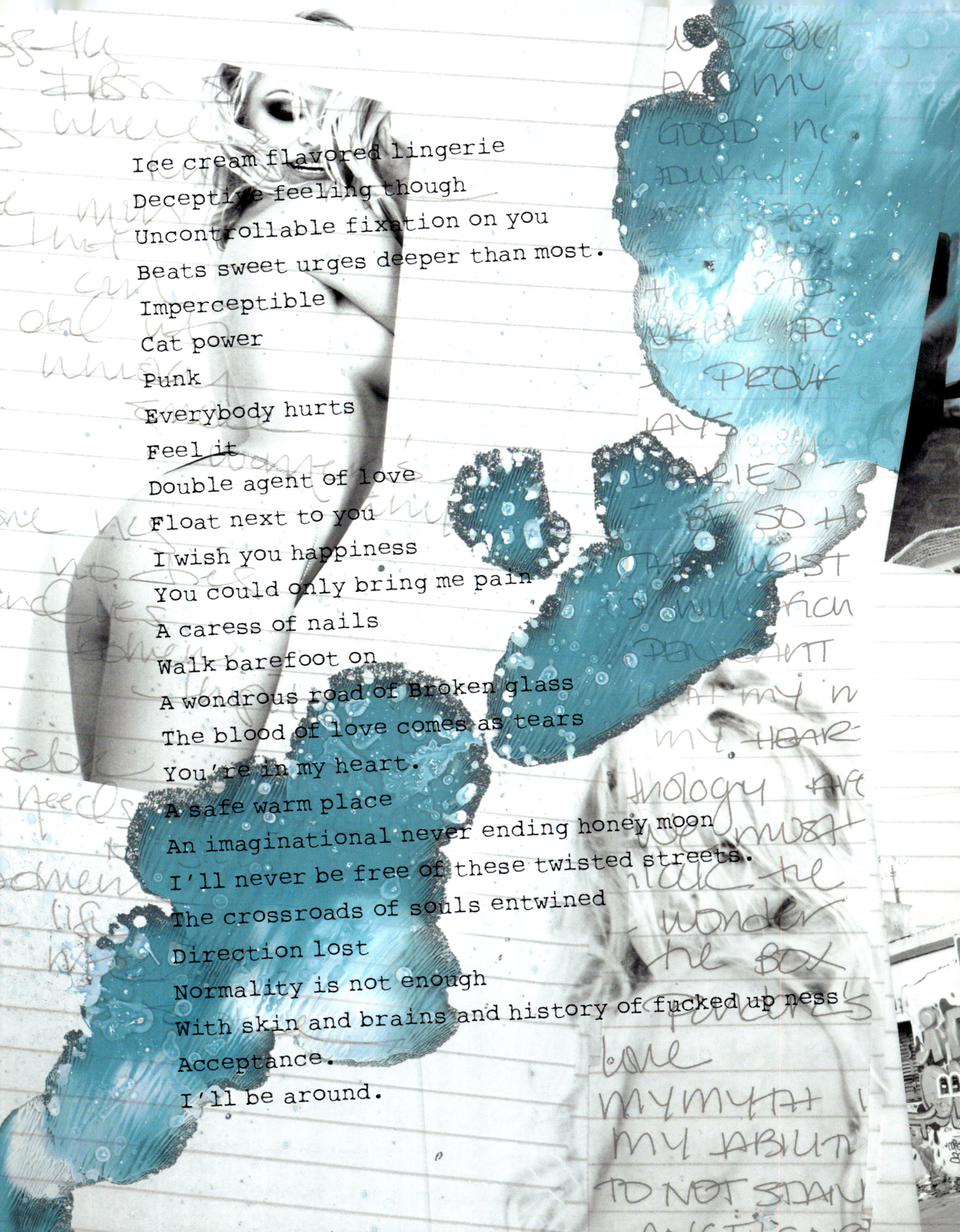

Ice cream flavored lingerie
Deceptive feeling though
Uncontrollable fixation on you
Beats sweet urges deeper than most.
Imperceptible
Cat power
Punk
Everybody hurts
Feel it
Double agent of love
Float next to you
I wish you happiness
You could only bring me pain
A caress of nails
Walk barefoot on
A wondrous road of Broken glass
The blood of love comes as tears
You're in my heart.
A safe warm place
An imaginational never ending honey moon
I'll never be free of these twisted streets.
The crossroads of souls entwined
Direction lost
Normality is not enough
With skin and brains and history of fucked up ness
Acceptance.
I'll be around.

Disuelve a Las Reinas
Reina de Brujas

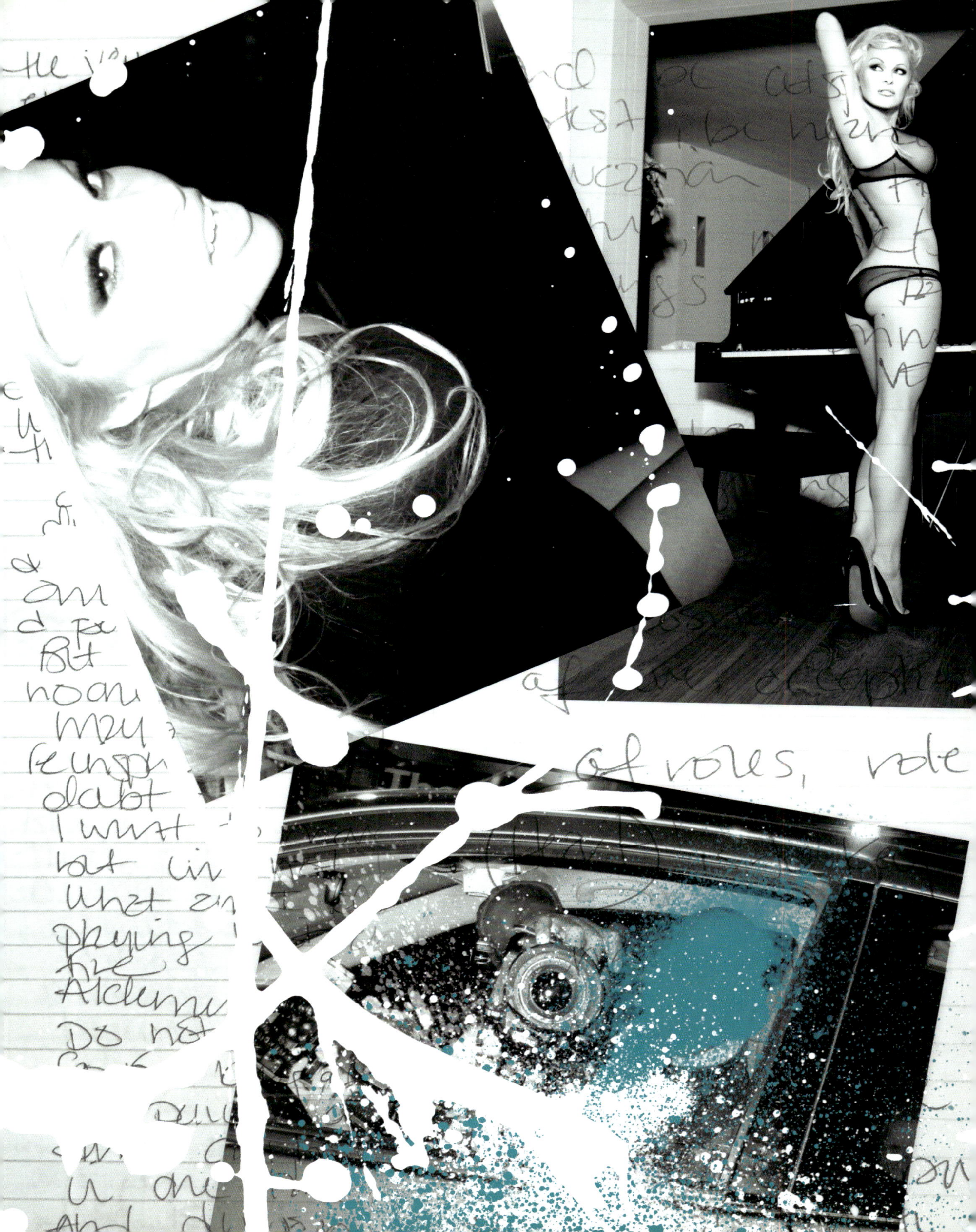

County line
A spot in time.
An amber blue sunset
For you.
A love unrealized. A wait, a step, a patient prayer.
If it takes forever
I'll be there
I don't want to love you . . .
Not now
I don't.
But want is a strange word. It's a nagging self-serving
word . . . I want, I want . . . is just for me . . .
So not that word . . . Give is better.
Need is too . . . I don't want to be another one who
needs you.
Desire is one thing I dare not do
A fantasy . . . playful . . . but thoughts create power.
A burning hope . . .
A smoke signal-visualize
I see you at the end of my bed . . . head in hands-
It's ok.
I don't want to be a Dr. Seuss . . . He always jumps in my
head. The places you'll go.
Green eggs and ham.
He was a genius . . .
Bukowski too.

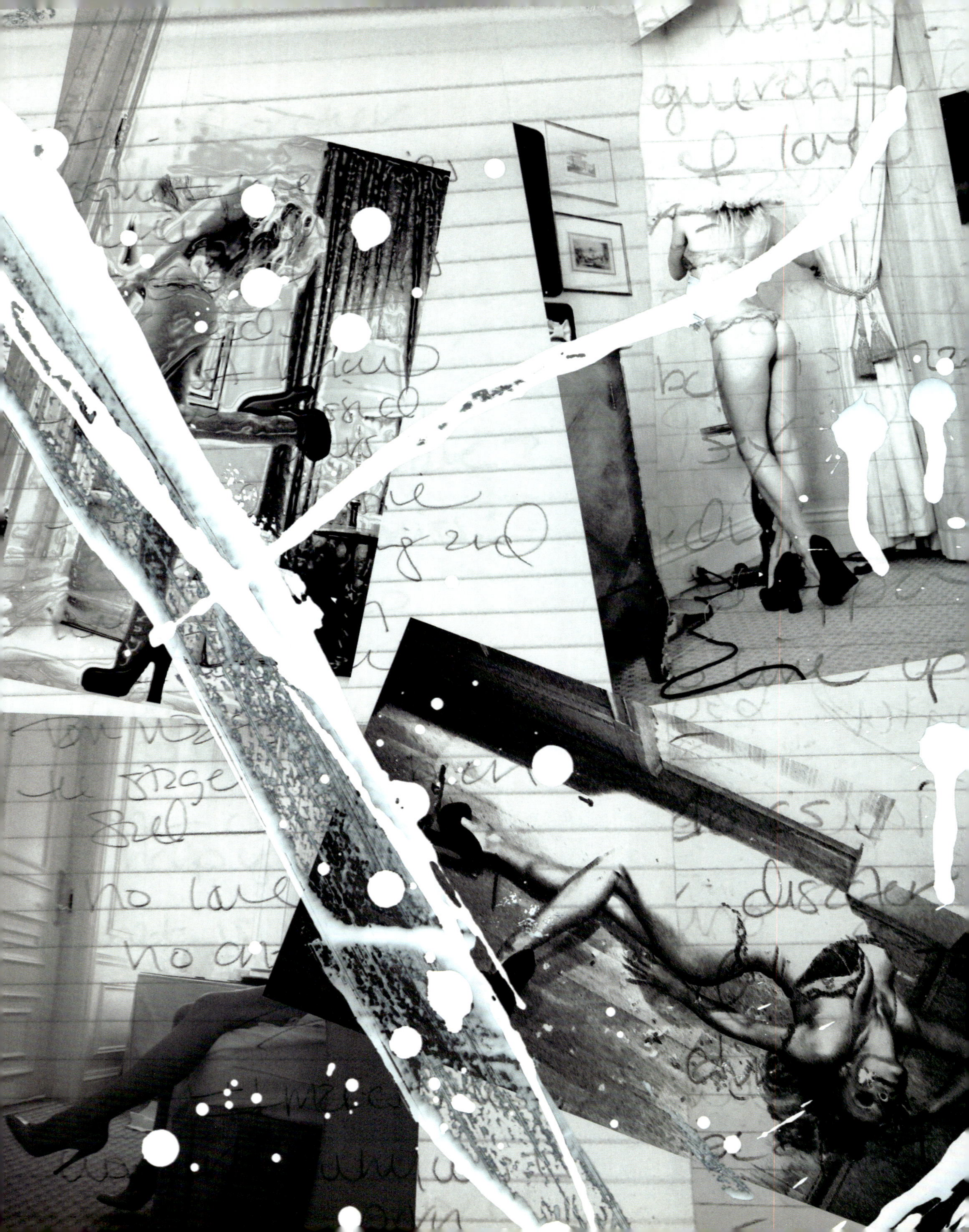

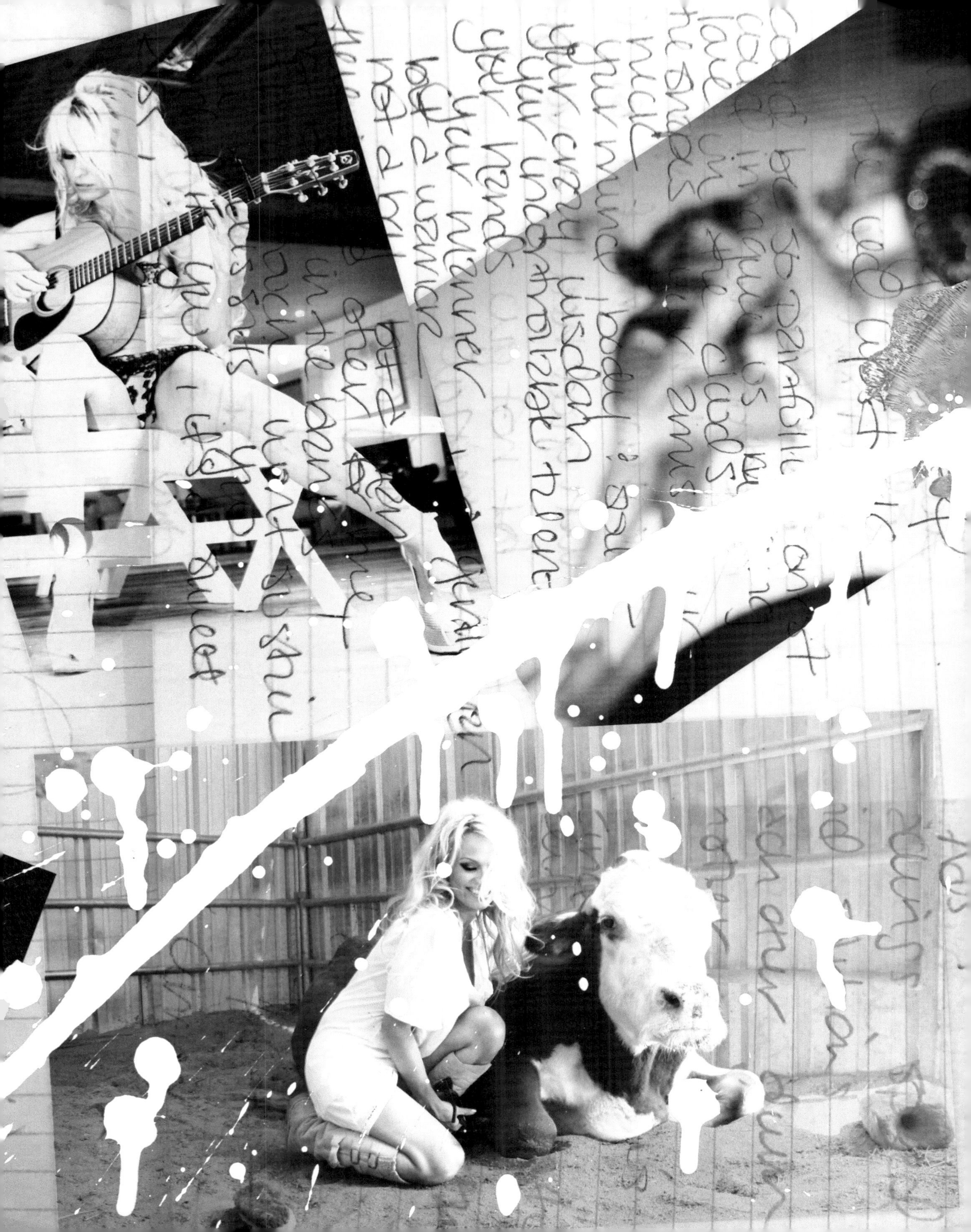

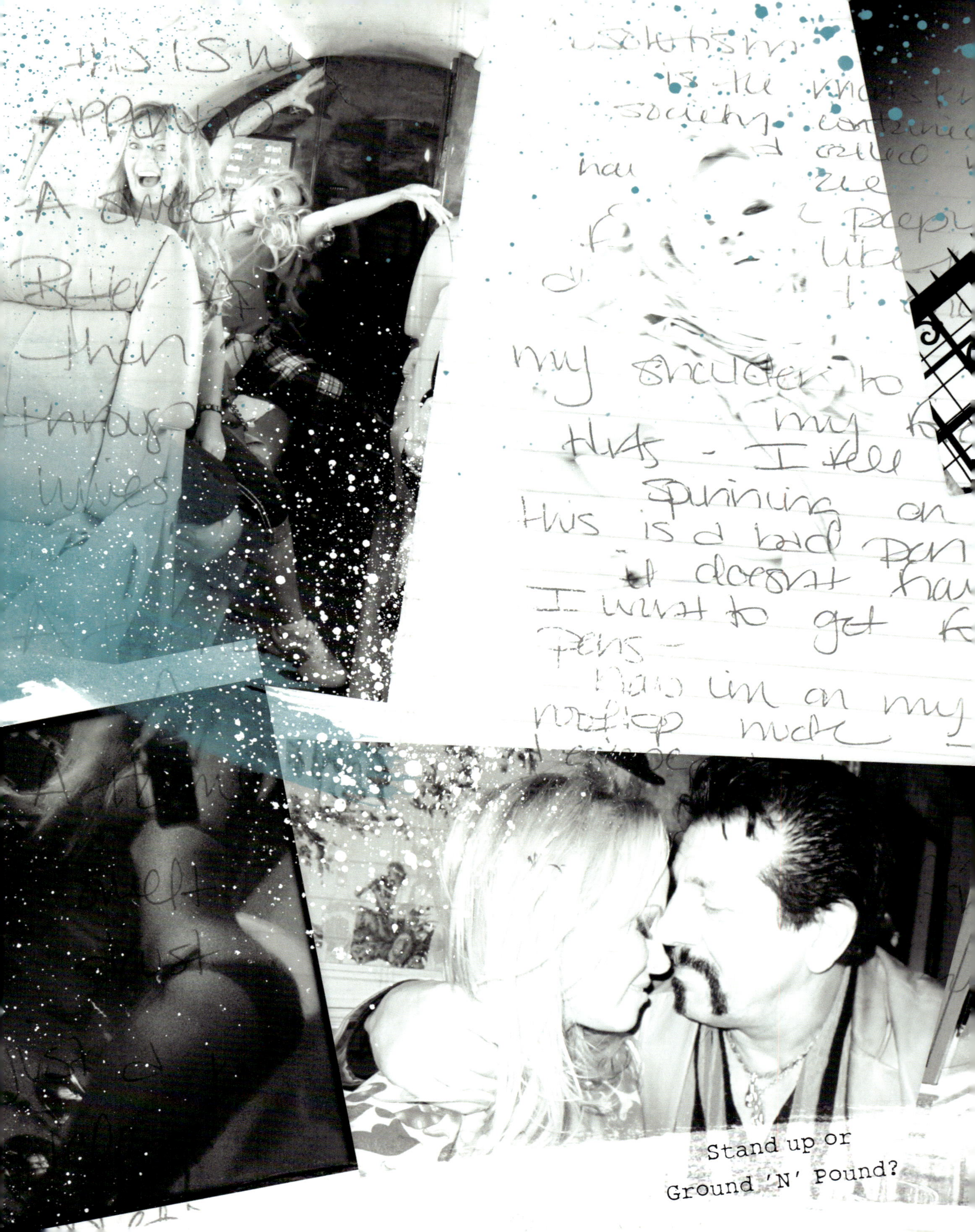
Stand up or
Ground 'N' Pound?

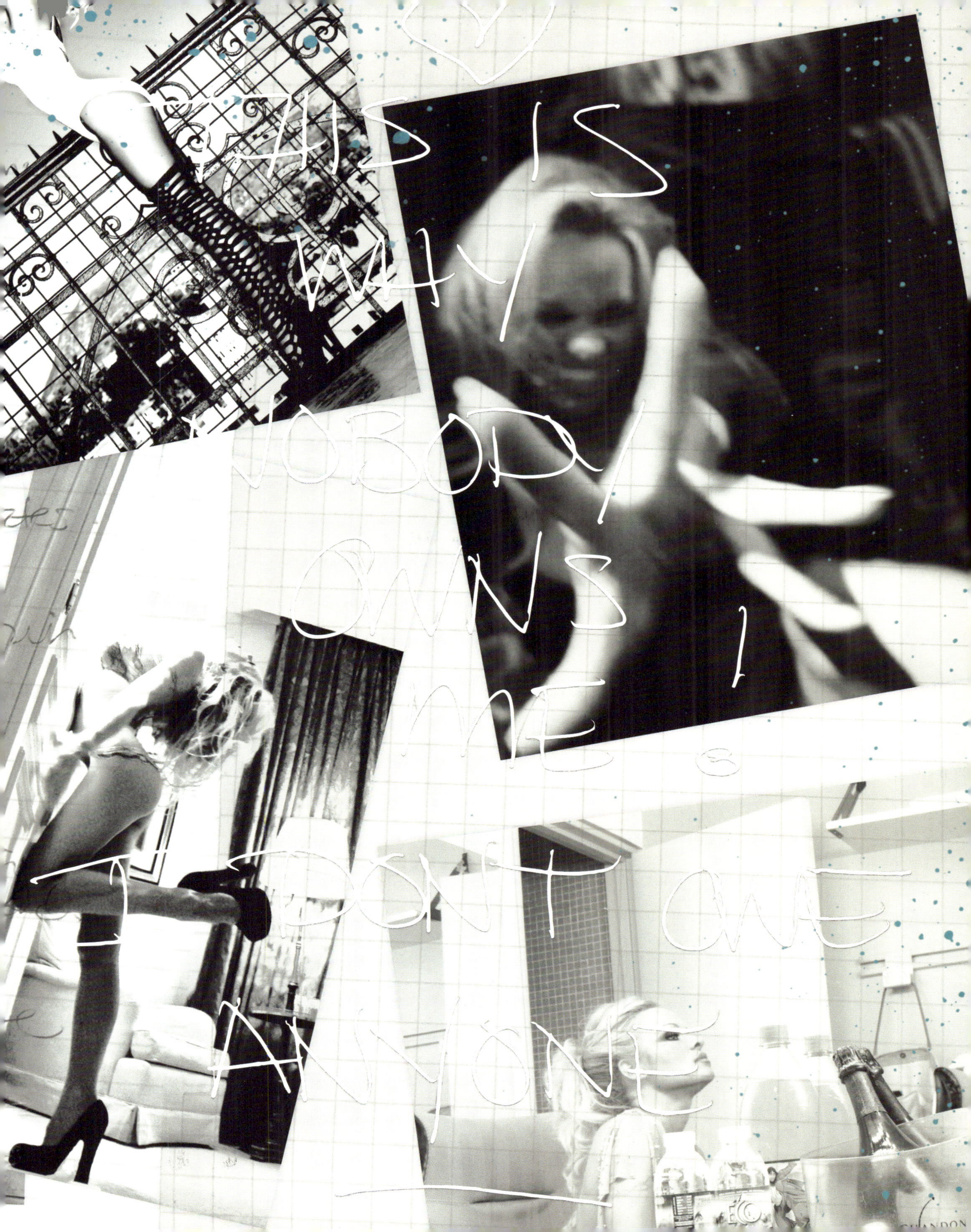
THIS IS WHY
NOBODY OWNS ME
I DON'T OWE ANYONE

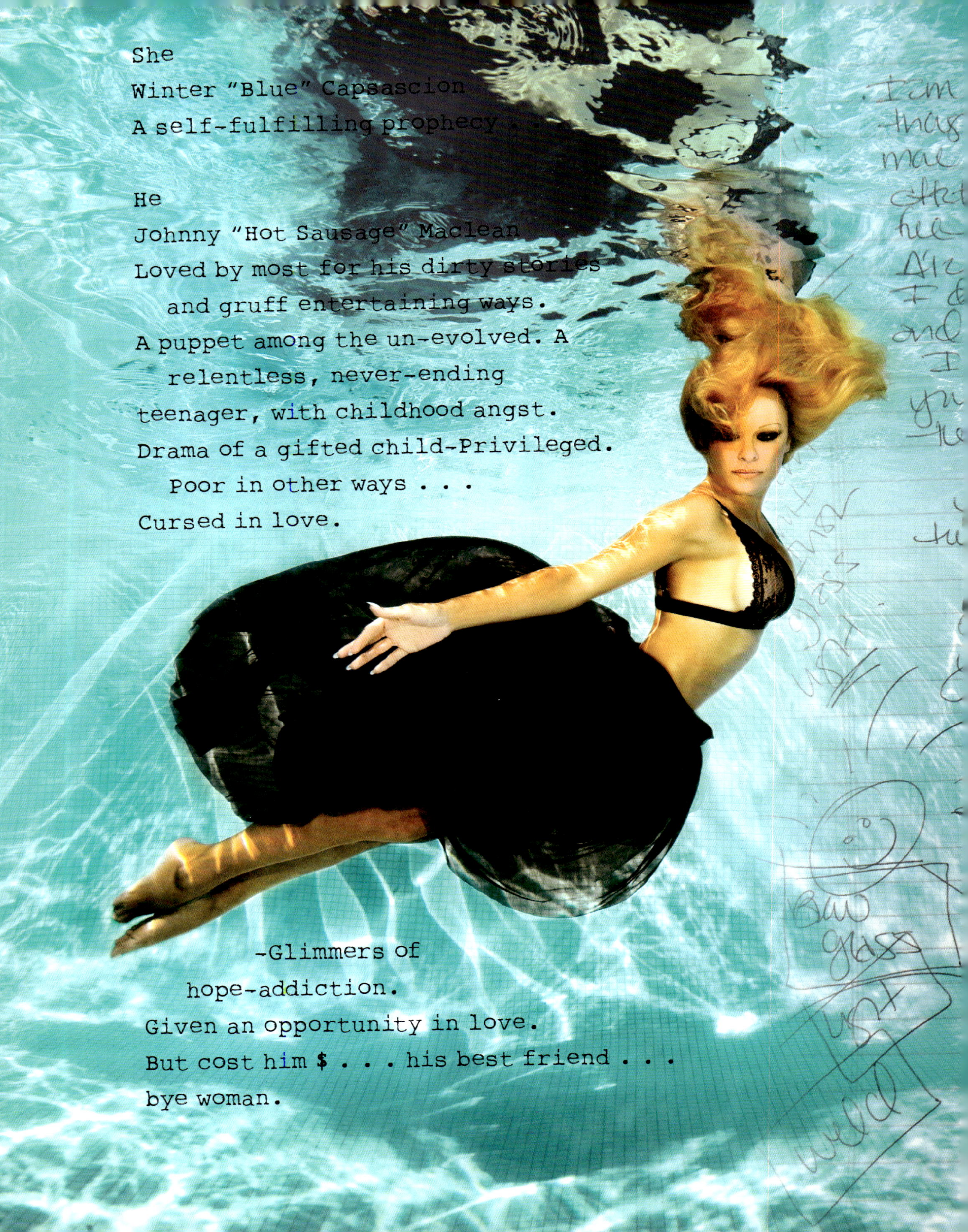
She
Winter "Blue" Capsascion
A self-fulfilling prophecy .

He
Johnny "Hot Sausage" Maclean
Loved by most for his dirty stories
    and gruff entertaining ways.
A puppet among the un-evolved. A
    relentless, never-ending
teenager, with childhood angst.
Drama of a gifted child-Privileged.
    Poor in other ways . . .
Cursed in love.

    -Glimmers of
    hope-addiction.
Given an opportunity in love.
But cost him $ . . . his best friend . . .
bye woman.

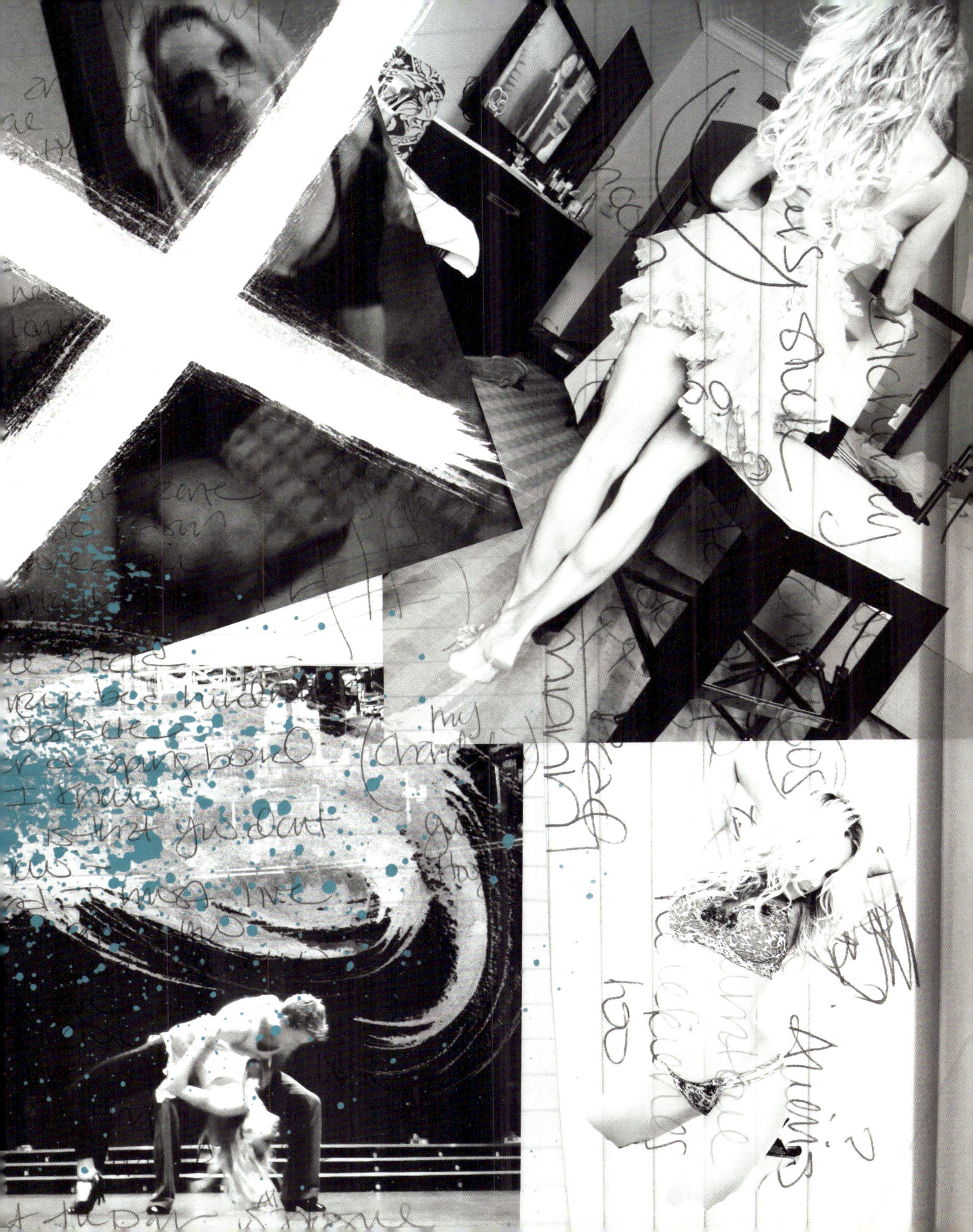

The intensity is
    different . . . I feel you in
    my bones . . . the core of my
    being . . .
    you resonate . . .
I have my encounters, my
    friendships. My writing
    to them is different . . .
    Hardly poetic, I'd say . . .
    forced? You-it just comes
    and comes . . . I'm mostly
    alone . . . With this smokey
    blue jazz bar in my head,
    glamorous split gown,
    tanned oiled legs, blonde
    curls . . . glossed
    mouth . . . I write, I play
    jazz, I make balloon
    animals . . .
I get closer to who I am-when
    I'm torturing myself.
You are a torture . . . yet,
This is purely innocent . . .
    I hope you take it that way
    . . . You don't want me-I'm
    sure of it . . .
We might just kill each
    other . . .
But, thank you for your . . .

unique friendship . . .
    your golden ear . . . Thank
    you for not hurting me. Or
    squashing my spirit . . .
I couldn't bear it . . .
    I've been stupid too many
    times . . . here I am . . .
    again. Sabotage . . .
You have left your mark
    on me . . .
I'm grateful . . . I won't
    forget . . .
I shall be more realistic-
I know some good men. Suitors
    aside . . . I'm such a
    rebel . . . with my
    choices . . .
I should be so lucky . . .
I'm refocusing . . . but . . .
    you're such a gentleman . . .
You are in charge . . . I must
    start a life with
    someone . . . asleep in
    lavender . . .
My fantasies don't end . . .
I most obviously love you . . .
Why do I keep being taken
    away . . .

says u love
a person
not ... idea
characters have come
and physio-paths
in the
... - Dream at
my ...) -
... are still
... us

participate in the
the joys and sufferings
of life -
I will die a servant
not a ...

I dont ... what to
do with ... this
I know how to avoid,
create,
susta...

keep ... ... sure
I dont ... this

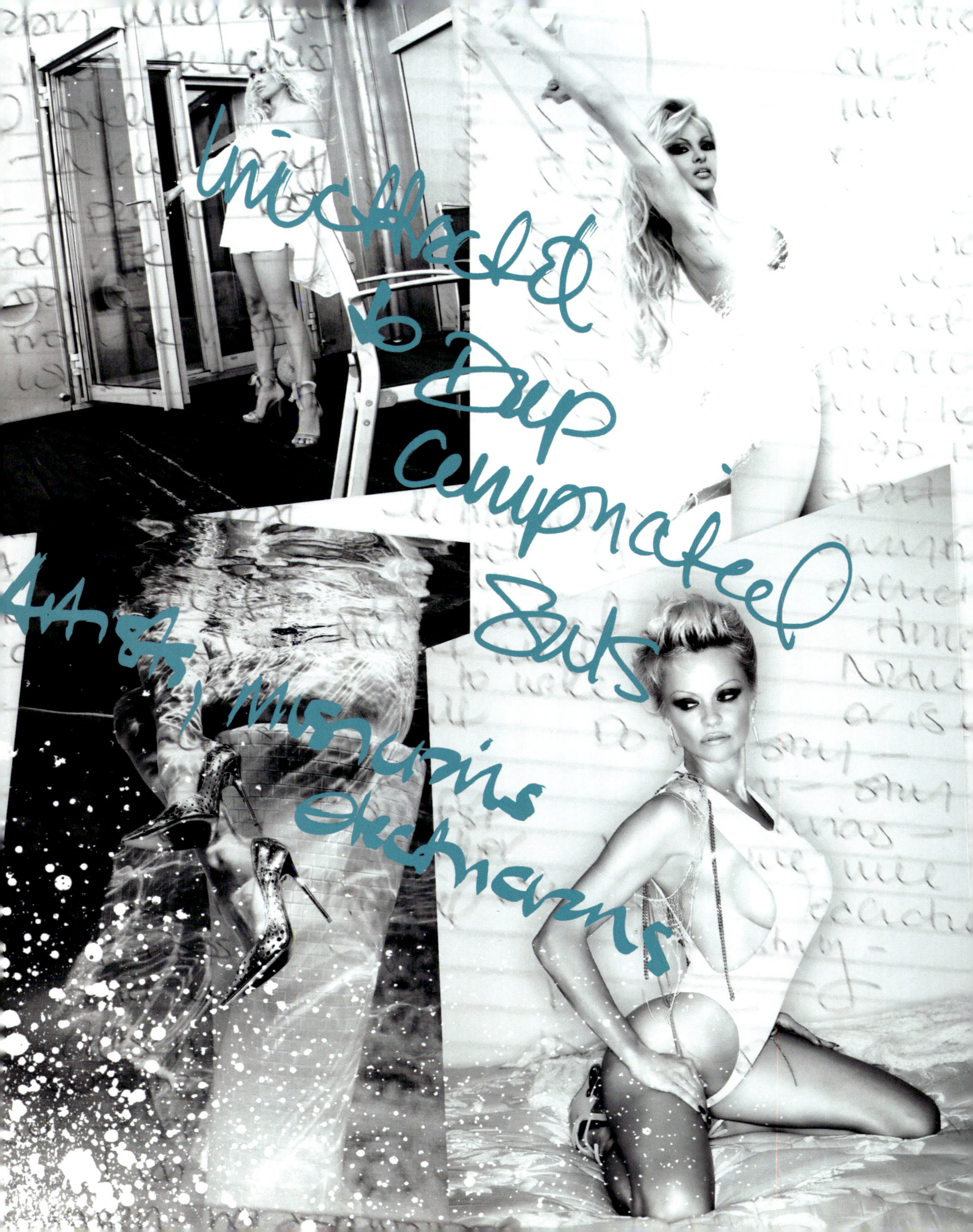

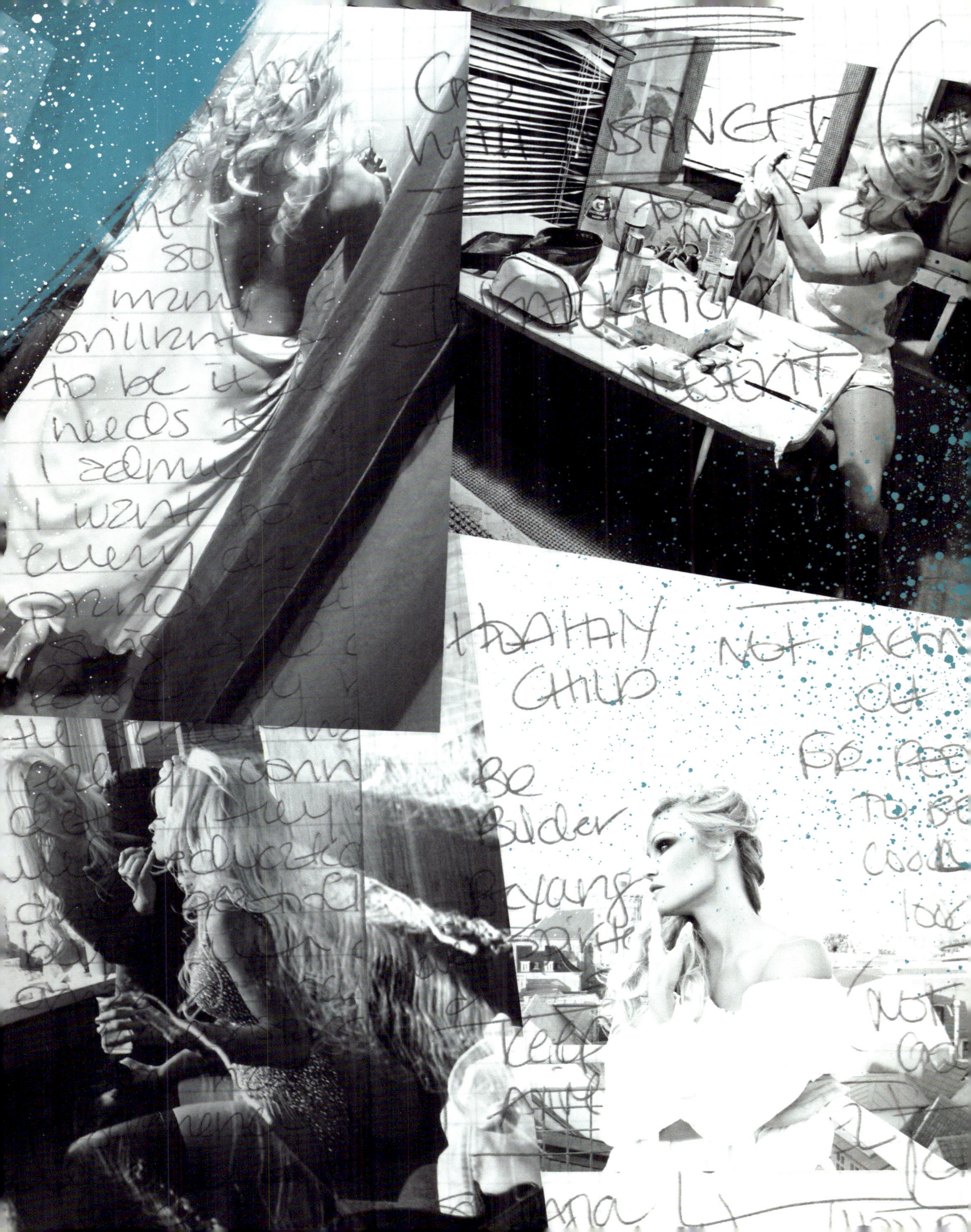

with a long ribbon
[illegible] poodle
[illegible] was behind her back

[illegible] buying
[illegible] deeply
first
[illegible] een with envy
[illegible] loosing
freeness
[illegible] ing
[illegible] deles —
[illegible] out ad [illegible]

[illegible] here
[illegible] es
[illegible] ingenuous to
[illegible] es
[illegible] not going
[illegible] is
she looks da[illegible]
her feet
[illegible] beanie
[illegible] her toes

[illegible] music singing
[illegible] people is da[illegible]
a range [illegible]

[illegible] door the [illegible]
[illegible] ts — drunken, u[illegible]

[illegible] ppearing
[illegible] me a not
[illegible] o true imp[illegible]

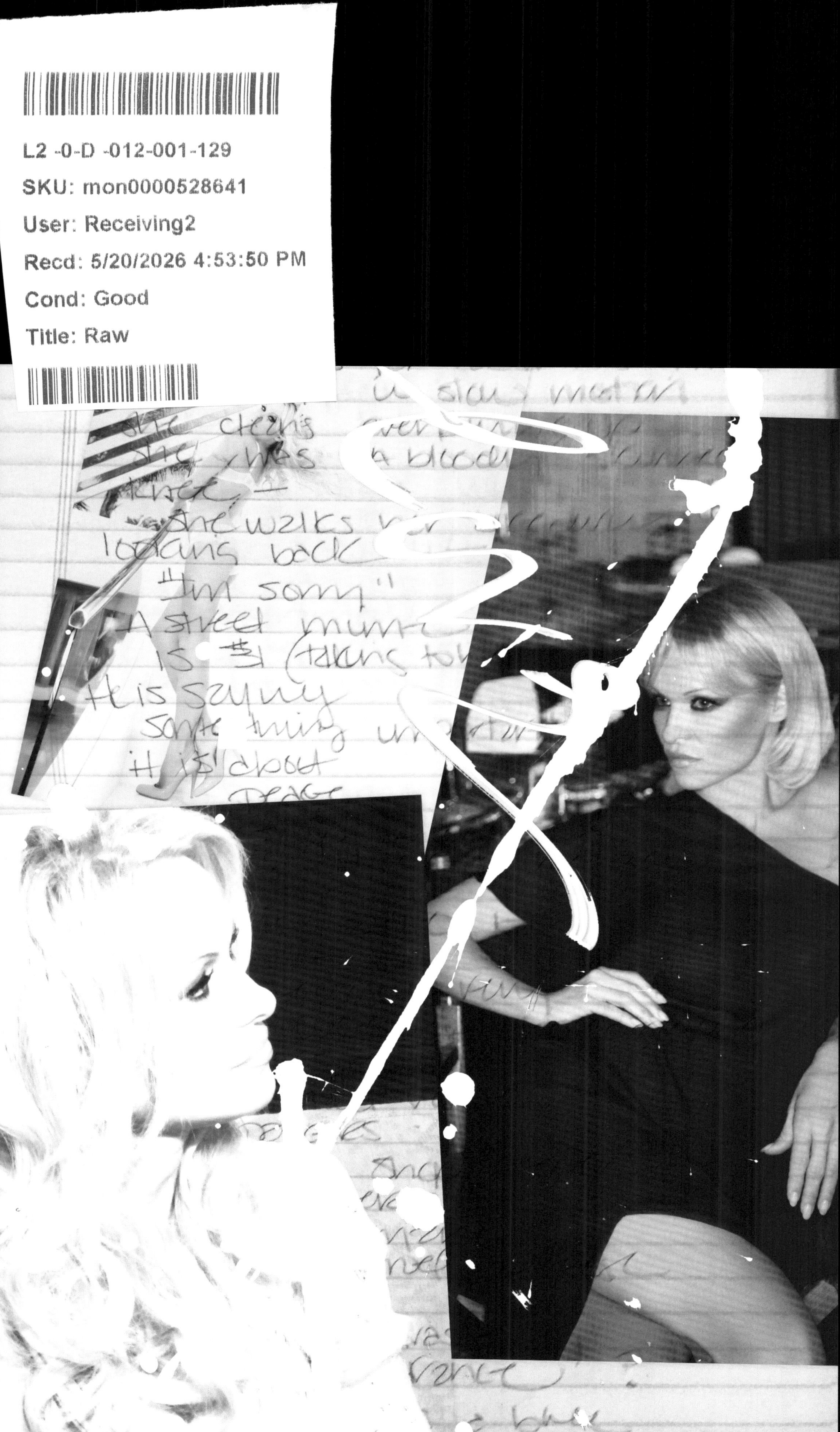

Here I am
Now full of staples, not 1 or 3.
The least exposed
Part of me.
My mind, my conflicted reasoning,
    my way . . .
I Change,
depending on the day.
Why am I always in love . . .
With thin air . . .

...es, broken.
...s, blood, a
sitting at my
side, thousand
graves, restlessly
I search for
the answer - it
is nowhere near
me... the
...

...ing of ...
...s to ...
...e world ...
lovers -
... and be
unconsistent
manhood -
...ishness and
class
political people.
...there and
...utiful people
lead in
the world?
I don't
think ... ...
if beauty
comes from
inside...

the lovers
banquet. I
...ited enough
I miss the
world - the
ocean, laughter
peace - a warrior
A gentleman's
...ch...
it doesn't
...

...exterior they
really
think
... the

and
I dream -
...were

lost.

[illegible handwritten text]

— it is too
[illegible] to be during you
[illegible] work
[illegible] is too dangerous —
[illegible] too all too long
[illegible] the arms to stab [illegible]

A troubled heart.
Choices I need you to make.
I can see the outcome.
But . . .
I don't want to hurt you. I
see you're a winner. I'm
who'll lose.
And I'm not playing games.
Just existing down the
street. I only write
when I have to. My
thoughts are constant.
A flow. More than you
should know. They veer
to here and there. They
aren't sensible. They
are somehow appreciated
though. I'll stay my way
for awhile. Not sure
where to land. Circling
the runway.
I wonder if this makes
sense. If I let you
lead this. It will be
a sexual fling like
we've had before. I
need provocation. The
magic of loves twists
and turns. I have to
stay alone. My boys
need my full attention.
Somehow I know where
I'm headed. But this
is too quick. Too much.
Too wrong. Not right.
I need direction. The
director. Where is he.
Call me.

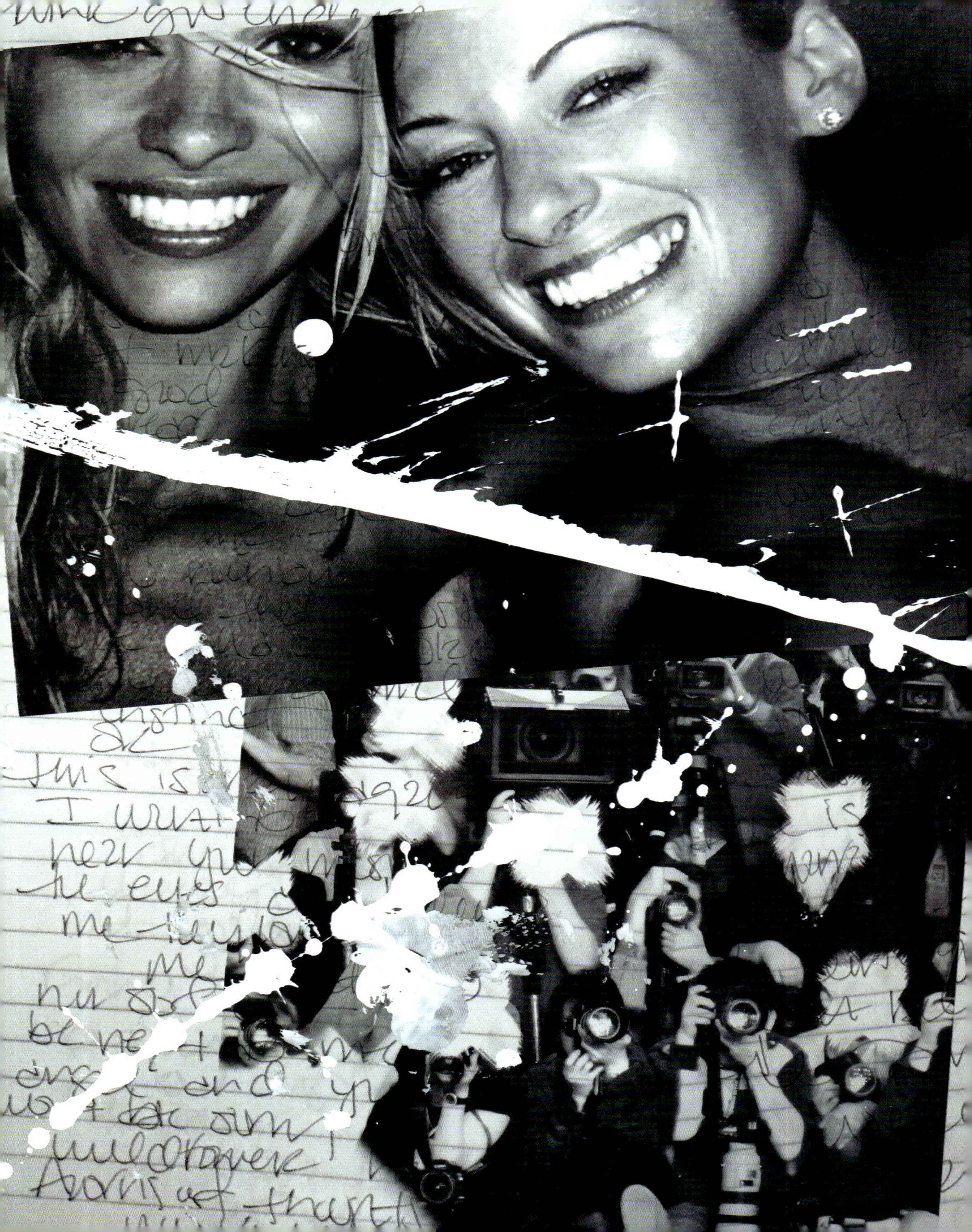

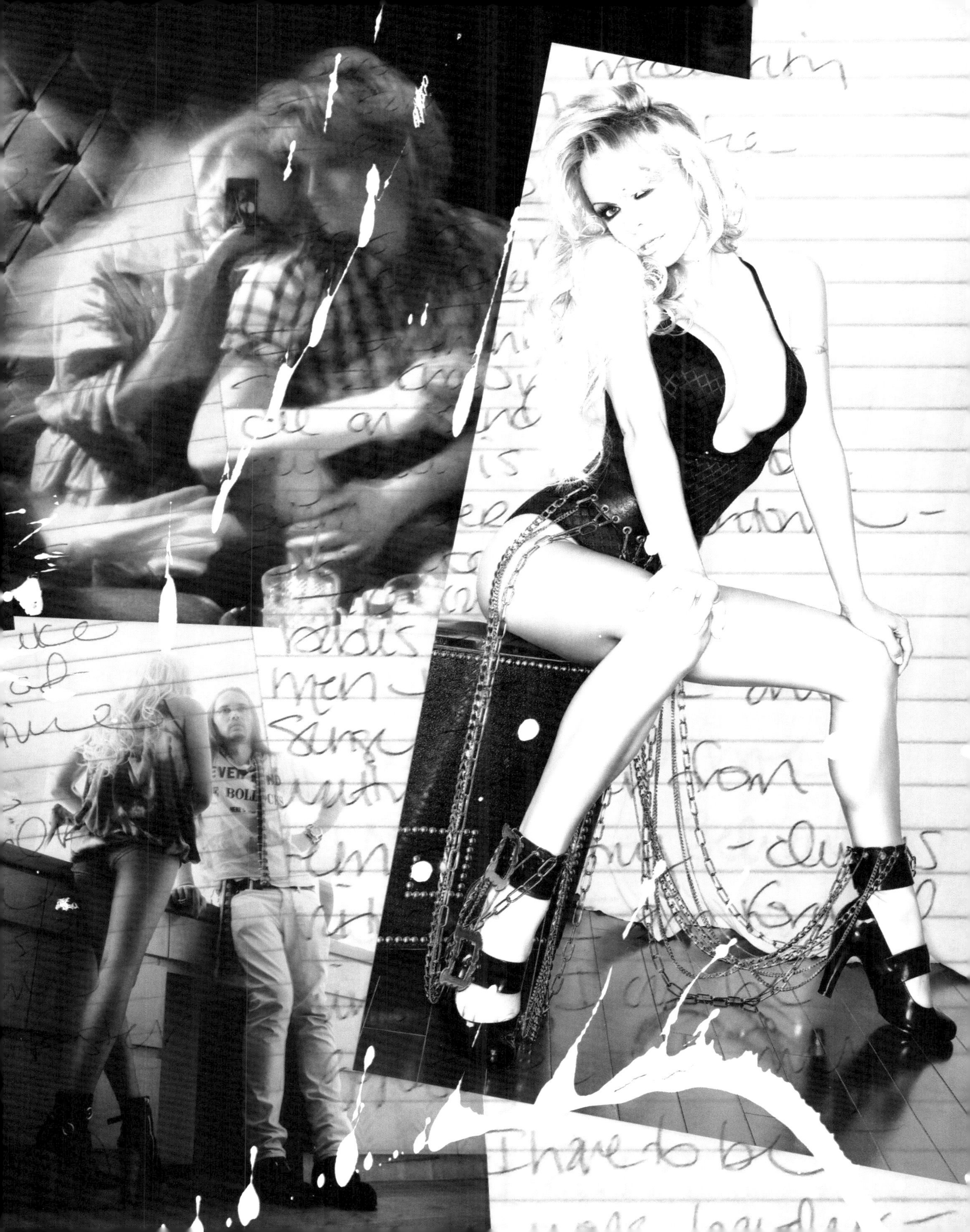

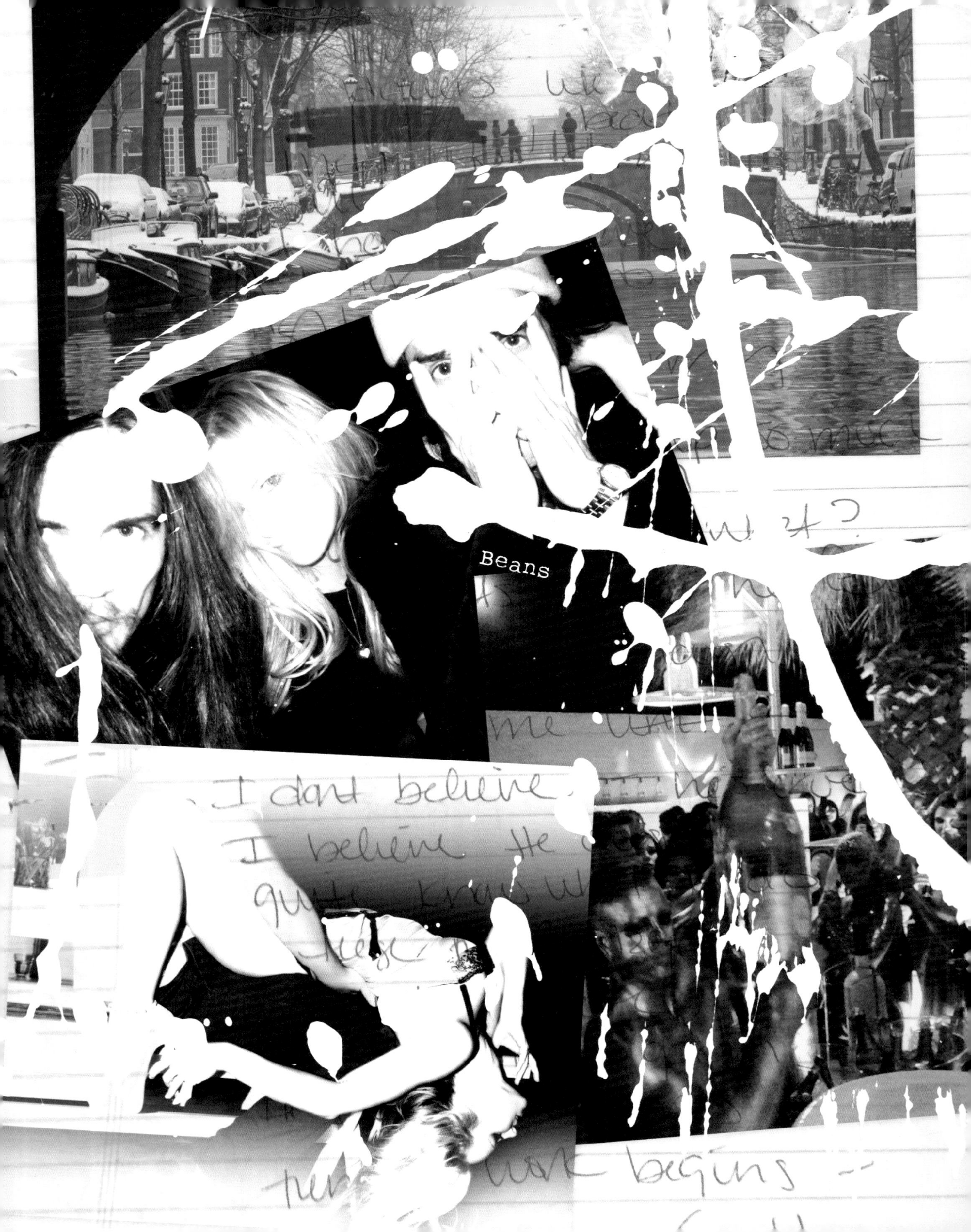

Beans
I dont believe
I believe the
quite know wh

[illegible] of hope —

I didn't know I am
[illegible] lifestyle
I don't [illegible] the [illegible]
SEX [illegible]
[illegible] magazine
[illegible] feel like
a woman [illegible] very

[illegible]
[illegible] te [illegible] was ing to [illegible]
[illegible] no[illegible] todo — [illegible]
[illegible] day mun[illegible] as chunk[illegible]
wet bed
sun su[illegible]
sand [illegible] malibo
[illegible]son in love
[illegible]
[illegible] part [illegible]ween mant[illegible]
[illegible]
[illegible]nald [illegible]
A

My life as
funny
laughter
Requiem
when [illegible]

the desacri[illegible]
touches
of med[illegible]

the [illegible] of
[illegible] ausin
me wit[illegible]
the si[illegible]
sell — the su[illegible]
the [illegible]
[illegible]
and

do you objectivity this
connect ... to human silk
... Geisha
... spiritualize their
music
intelligent classical
price (rich) proportions
met (self) (listen) NO
I understand tattoos.
we have had or ...
good time new ... hope!
... (am)
... beautiful ...
... make love
... to write I found
... licorice

I have made others
I have had my babies
they are growing up
you have had yours
And they
Are beautiful —
Everything is warm &
Everything is ripe

A lucid
dream.
A lucid true
you know what to
do next
the feeling not
B real
Believing in
sweet mind
want my own
not what
unusual me
but maybe you don't

To look after myself
And the work
I do for animals
And the environment

is never a beginning
life moves mysteriously
through everywhere but

the love waits our

the moon

RESPOND

heart and pray,
they will somehow
this and my must.
they know they die le...
...ded it... they
lived a long que...
have accepted hi...
like a nature en...
maybe pain is easi...
died sick... wasn't he...

A... content
...
the disc...
...my...
the di...
...nk...
...words that's
tell our...
every's re...
...nce
time for ... act
...appearanc...
...acceptance
forgiveness
so we can tr...
live at ar d...
why did god n...
...for money
or spite
or wrong
I was made as...
to encourage he...
men
to lift them up a...
praise them
give strength
and nourishment...

...aren't give...
to... to stop at table —
a plant for red carp...
behind
—
— mamishell helping

Smoldering . . .
I know it's bad for you . . .
But, this is when I wish,
I had a cigarette-
something I've never tried-(light up)
some kind of relief . . .
I wish it were Italy forty years ago-
The moon rising over the Amphitheater-
to tremendous applause . . . . (clap)
Europeans don't seem to care about silly
smoking laws?
We do what we want anyway-
behind closed doors-
Our true character, collective complexi-
    ties,
childish activities-
patterns-genetics? Attention deficit-
. . . SEX . . . a lost art-a sickness-
perversions-
Lost sensuality-
The cruel smell of orange blossoms . . .
I love being in love-but expectations,
make it impossible to be happy-
or satisfied . . .
I've tried . . . so hard . . .

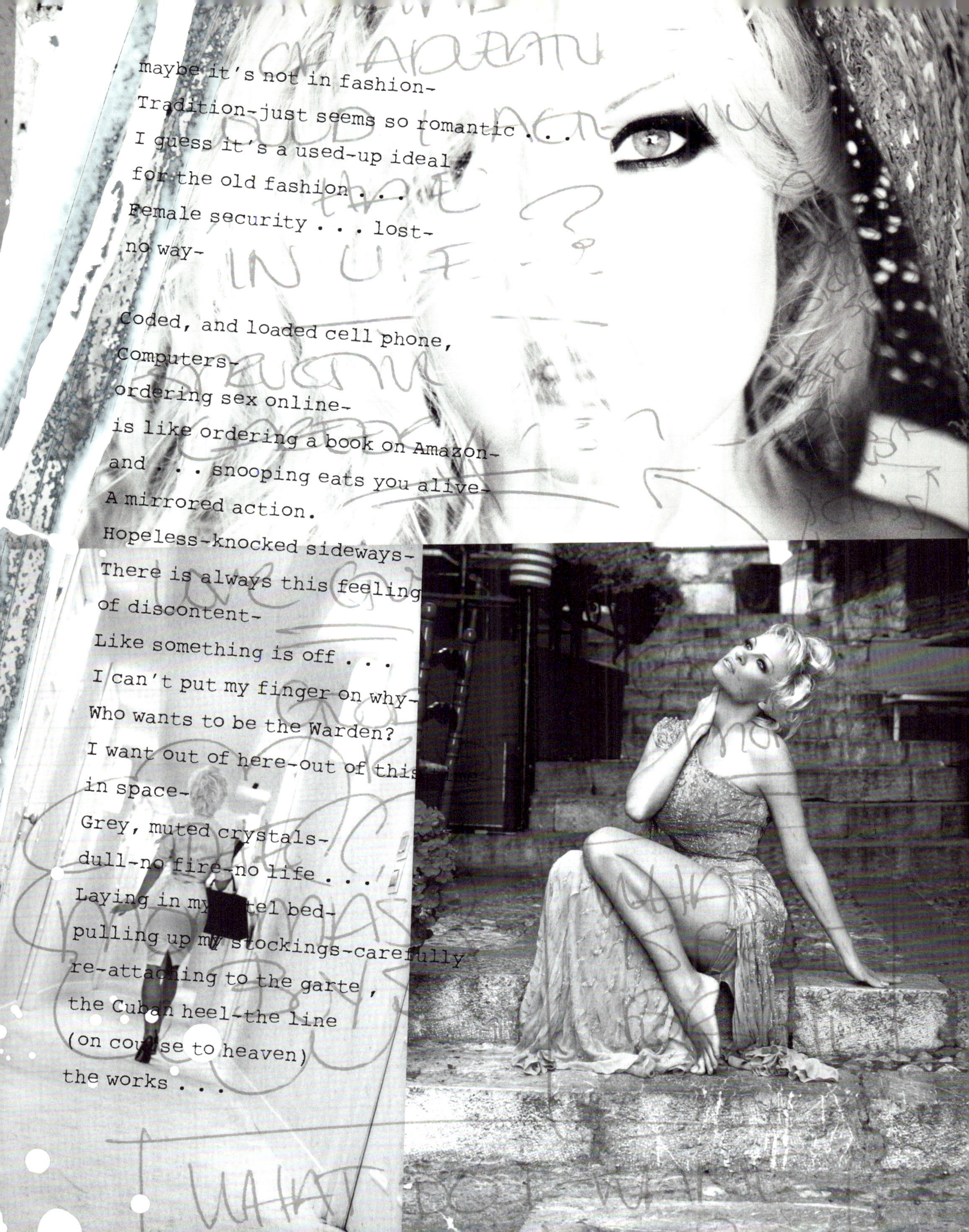

maybe it's not in fashion-
Tradition-just seems so romantic . . .
I guess it's a used-up ideal
for the old fashion . . .
Female security . . . lost-
no way-

Coded, and loaded cell phone,
Computers-
ordering sex online-
is like ordering a book on Amazon-
and . . . snooping eats you alive-
A mirrored action.
Hopeless-knocked sideways-
There is always this feeling
of discontent-
Like something is off . . .
I can't put my finger on why-
Who wants to be the Warden?
I want out of here-out of this . . .
in space-
Grey, muted crystals-
dull-no fire-no life . . . .
Laying in my hotel bed-
pulling up my stockings-carefully
re-attaching to the garter,
the Cuban heel-the line
(on course to heaven)
the works . . .

Feeling a little guilty-
I started to fantasize-
Il Postino, Pablo Neruda-
Should I go to Capri-?
So frustrated-
burning . . . questions . . .
No man knows what to do with me-
I blame myself-
To play with me is eternal-
I'm not "on the clock" or . . .
on the "payroll"-
rrrr-
I had to get out of the room-
The velvet stuff and porcelain things
closing in on me . . .
What have I done . . .
I knew it was wrong from the start-
impulsive base instinct . . .
Never dated a rich man . . . .
Euros from a vagabond . . .
Just start walking-(Like Jeanne
    Moreau)
(treadmill?)

Never look back-
There is only beauty ahead,
Salvation . . .
Glory
Rushing . . .
I almost forgot where I was-shit-
My white
Burberry trench-
-on the floor?
A parquet floor . . . (this could be
    real time now)
(Narration by a deep-voiced black guy)
BG-She stopped to admire its clever
    design,
ME-"So pretty"
BG-wrapped herself
She snuck out the door with a quiet
    click,
and seamlessly, floating down the hall-
    wire)
her Tom Ford feet didn't
touch the ground-

Falling gracelessly into an elevator
playing Nat King Cole's . . .
    "Stardust"?
(remembering the movie)
ME-"Fallen Angel?"
BG-Nobody was up yet-
out into the cool world she
    goes,
ME-"Freedom . . .
I can breathe . . ."
BG-looking for a
    little human
    contact?

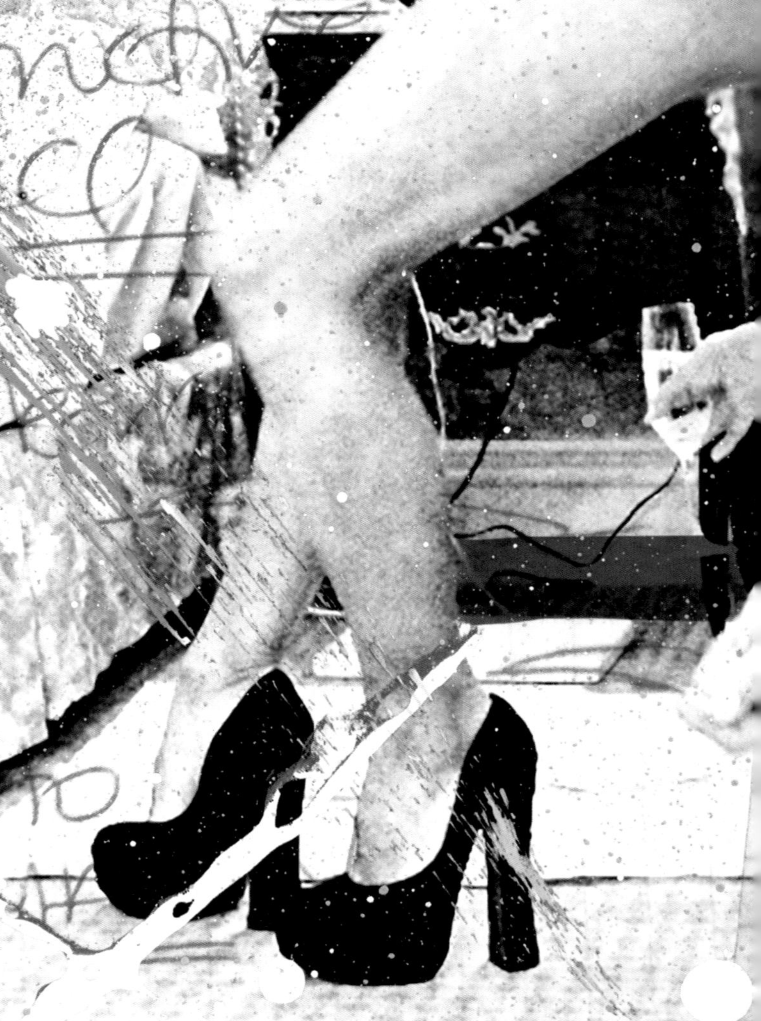

Playful
    seduction? . . .
ME-"I'm so hungry . . ."
BG-Her heart was racing-

It was barely dawn-
Bathed in perfect light-
magic hour . . .
ME-"Everyone looks good
    this early"

BG-Even cats
and hummingbirds
Was anyone watching her . . .

She gazed up into dark
windows . . .
to nobody . . .
and let the jacket fall loosely
around
her shoulders . . .

The rush coming back . . .
a little lost on purpose,
hiding around corners,
ME-"Dangerous-
my body is on fire-
my body is never done-trouble finds me-
please find me-
The iron is always hot!"
BG-She leaned against the cool wall of a
stony church-
It felt good, soothing-
ME-I wonder how prostitution works-
Does it ever feel good?
Lost little souls-being taken advantage
    of-

or taking advantage of-
Is it just for money? Is it
for attention?
or-both-
Women suffer-
Everywhere-
rules, rules,
rules-
conflicting
needs . . .
I can't find
the answers-
it's an epidemic-
I know I won't
compete with a
computer-
or-a gaggle of
Hollywood boys hiring
poor
Russian girls to swallow
loaves of bread
up their anuses?
or worse-sleep with fat hairy people?-
How does that work?"
BG-She was disturbed-
How far can she take this?-Is it even
    real?-
ME-"Have we lost men to thin air-
to the Abyss-
Flesh is attached to a heart and a brain
takes effort . . . and skill . . .
Where are the great lovers?-A lost art
    . . .
God, I hope not . . .
I've never been to Columbia-Should I
    go?"
Is this Hysteria? . . .
Objectification?
now-Coming down from the ceiling,
dripping in gold glitter-
Dancing with Nureyev-eyes closed-

the dream . . .
arousing my tenderness,
A sweet rawness-
feeling bruised and scratched up-
Hypnotic-
Life is sensual-not a "fix it in
    post"-
ME-I miss PLAYBOY-
The End of an Era-
Chivalry, elegance-
Celebrated imperfections-
differences . . . hot-passionate
    dreamy scenes . . .
The girl next door-shyness-"it's
    my first time''
but-not my last . . . (wink)
-I'm planning a mysterious coup-
Want to get in on it-
Julian Assange?
Is it healthy, to be fantasied
    about . . .
by many men-?
Isn't that the goal-
How many can we affect-
It's natural-to want to be de-
    sired-
The world creeps up on you-
and there you are,
ALL over the place-
places you never intended to be-
    (desert storm?)
(soldiers)
I am human you know-
left to adjust to the madness-
No mercy-pay the price-my fault
BG-feeling empty, sad-withdrawn-

Left to Isolate-Medicate.
Go to sleep-
ME-NO! I won't-
ME-You know-It's not freaky
    enough,
to just be beautiful-
I've never felt beautiful-
I always felt sexual . . . and
    blind . . .
oh wowwy . . . I'm losing my mind-
I'm shutting down-It's such a
    strange feeling . . .
going numb . . . in front of ev-
    eryone-
It's like a Self-inflicted
    drowning . . . hard to do-
(Alarm bells!!)-
When did I want to be this thing?-
To attract what?
When did I go from a curious lit-
    tle girl,
to an insatiable woman? Girl on
    the run . . .
Femme fatale . . . devoted
    and . . . divided.
Are we all going crazy? -
or, is it just me?
Is it that stuff on unwashed vege-
    tables?
When did I lose control over my
    own heart?-
When did I start believing,

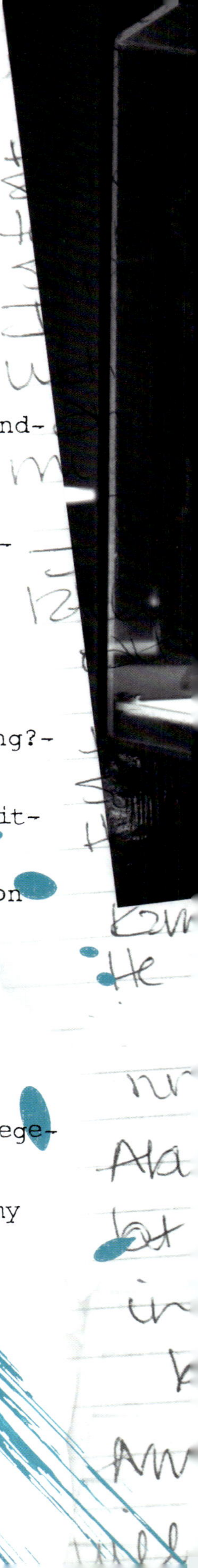

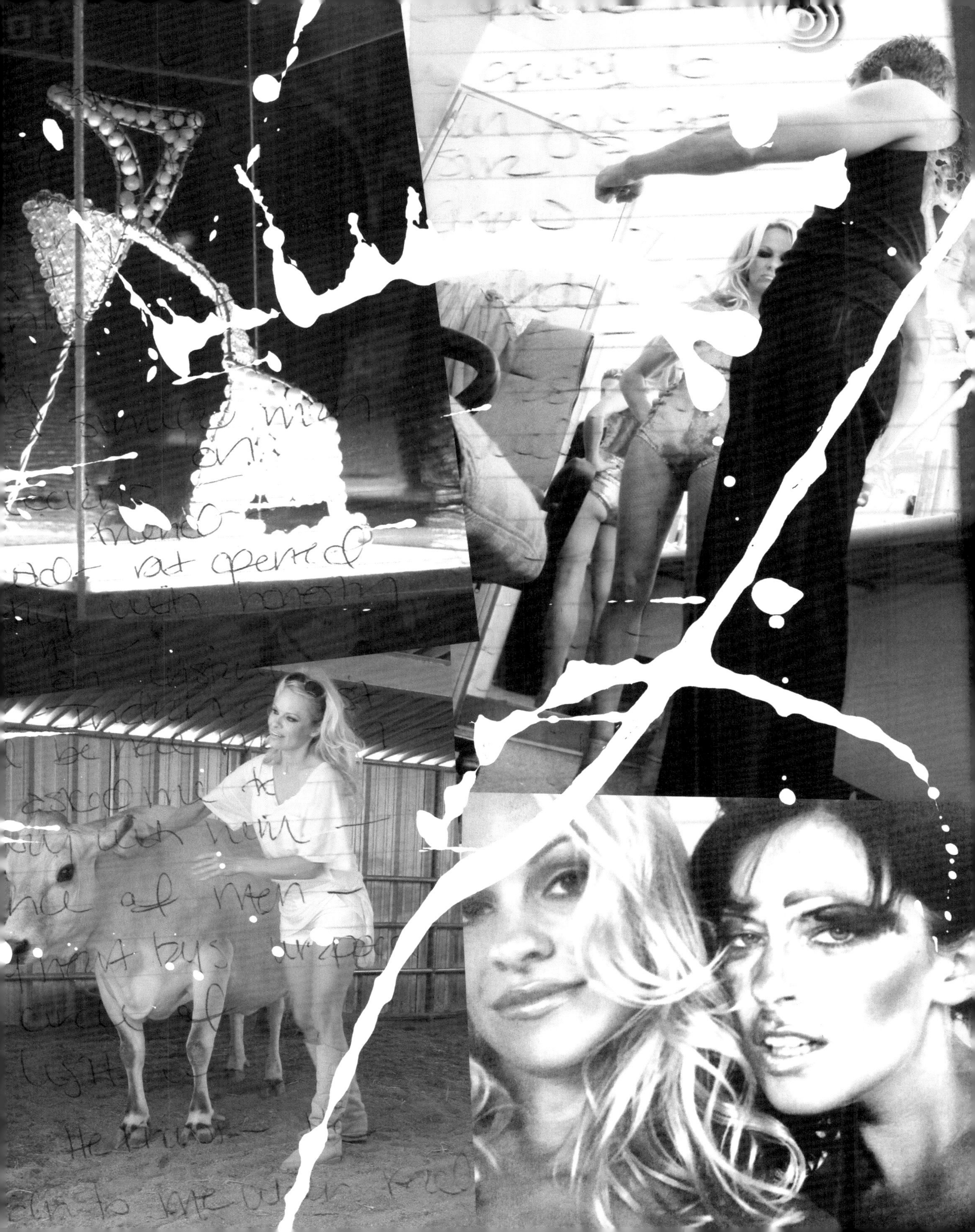

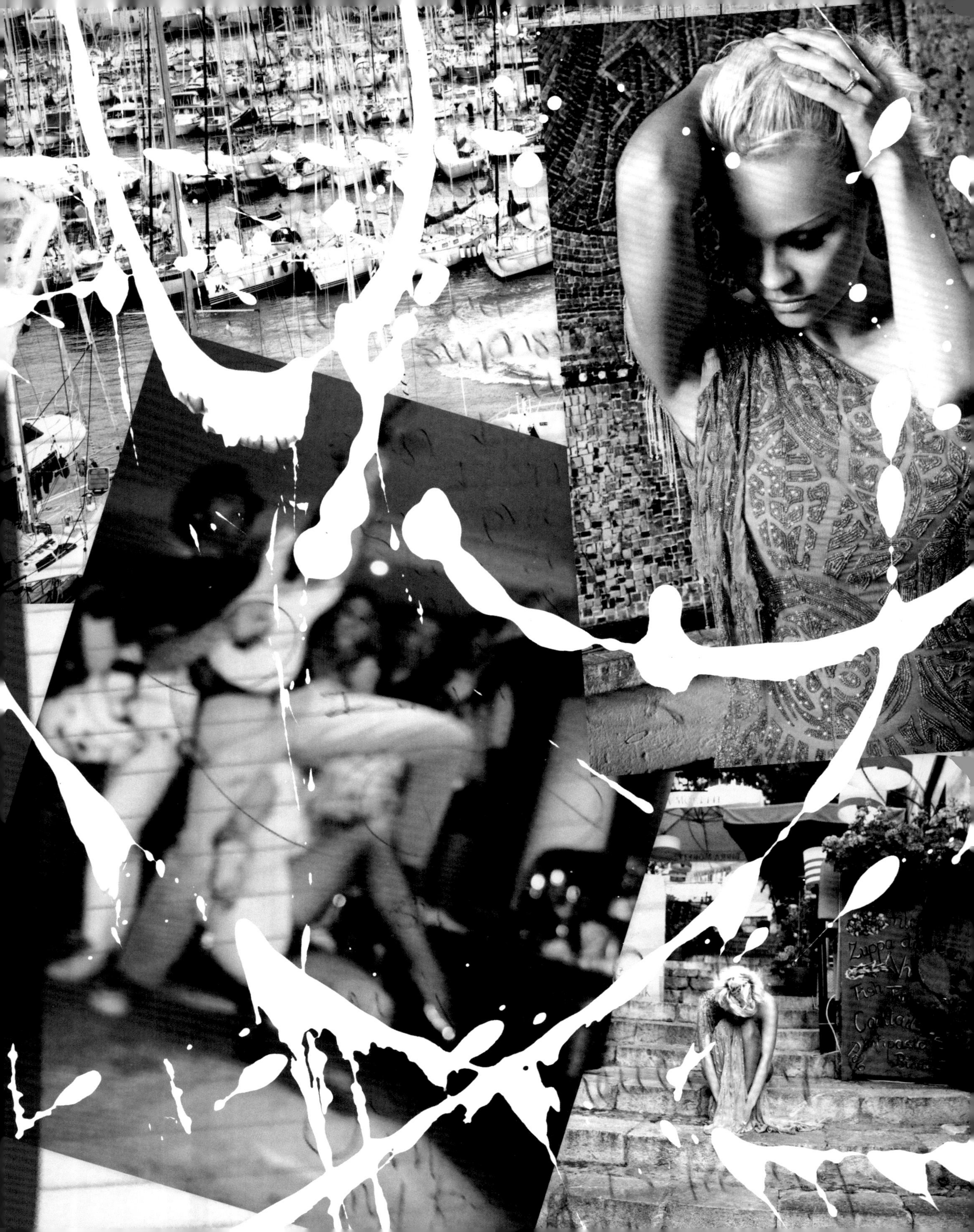

It doesn't feel good to
    be used, neglected,
    ignored-
controlled . . .
I'm not doing this-
It's humiliating-I have to
    turn this around-
Settling is powerless-
    desperate-
an illusion-
Can't buy your way out of
    this one . . . buddy!
I'm cold-
(She can't stop
    laughing . . .)

Reminds me of a play I
    wrote-
That one about The Hell's
    Angels,
starring-
Steve McQueen and Brigitte
    Bardot-

The Entr'acte . . .

* * A car chase-
She is going on and on (in

French) and
He's just trying to
    have his way with her-
    everything is double
    entendre Funny/
Sexy-(subtitles projected)
    they've stolen billions
    in diamonds-she's
    dripping
from head to toe . . . in
    a sparkly madness of
    laughter-60s Porsche-
    (or GT/Buillit
car?)
All in a car facing the
    audience-(with black
    and white projections
    from the 60s behind
    them) . . . They fall in
    love-
I'm not sure what The
    Hell's Angels have to do
    with it-but they stay in
    the title-
The End . . .

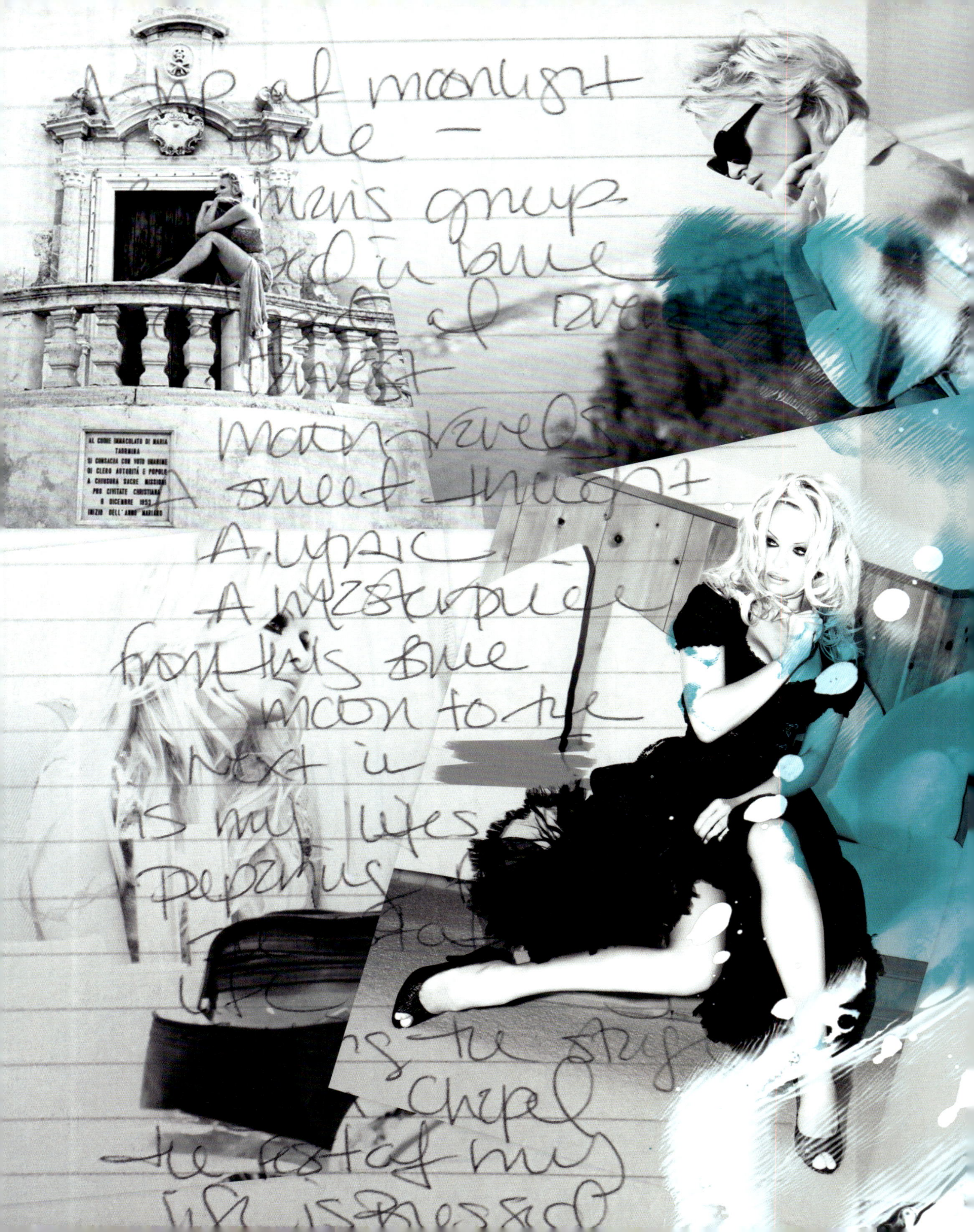
A ... of moonlight
blue -
marris group
in love
of love
harvest
moon drives us
A sweet incident?
A lyric
A masterpiece
from this blue
moon to the
next is
as my life's
departure

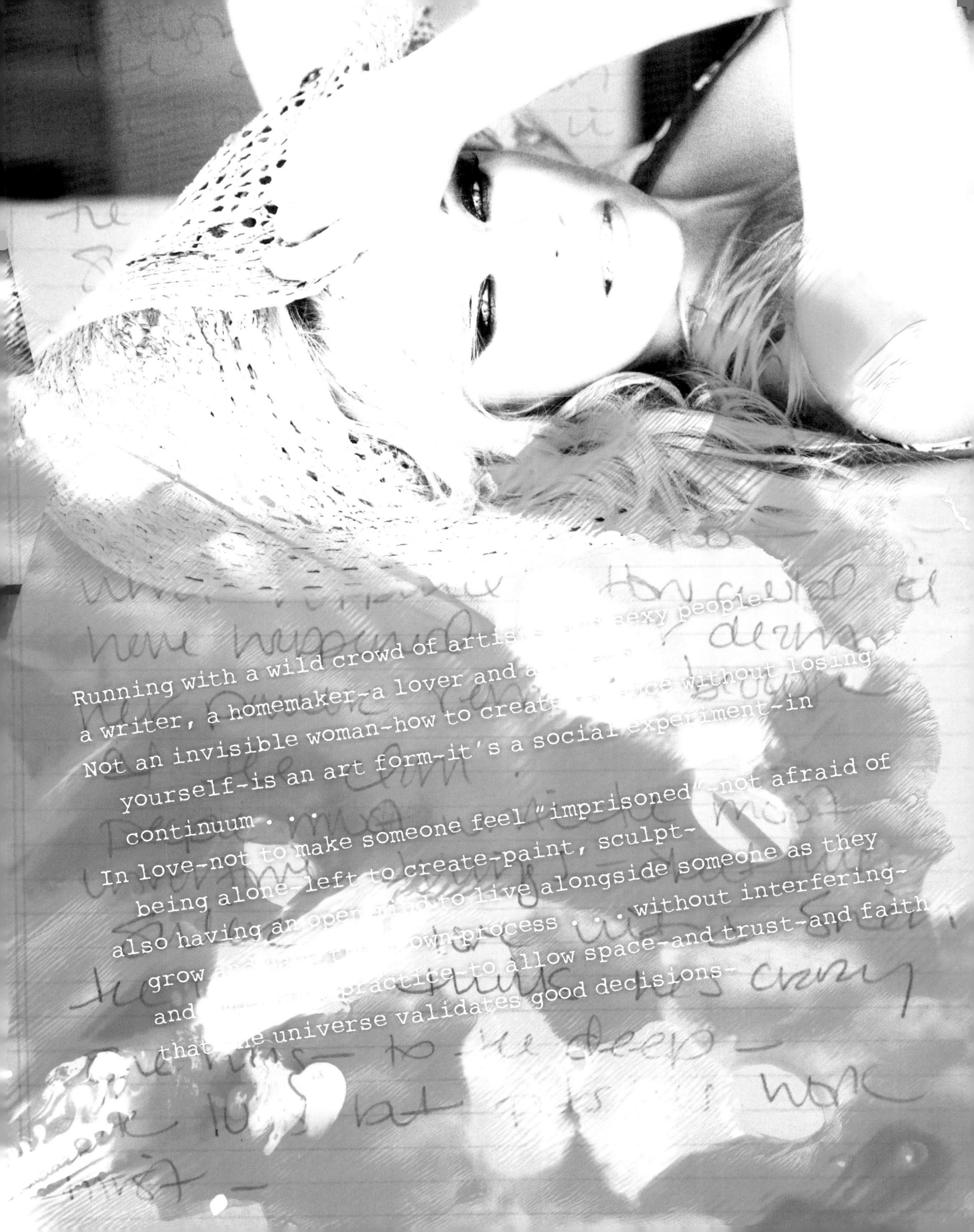

Running with a wild crowd of artists — sexy people
a writer, a homemaker—a lover and a ... ce without losing
Not an invisible woman—how to create ... yourself—is an art form—it's a social experiment—in
continuum • • •
In love—not to make someone feel "imprisoned"—not afraid of
being alone— left to create—paint, sculpt—
also having an open mind to live alongside someone as they
grow ... own process • • • without interfering—
and ... practice—to allow space—and trust—and faith
that the universe validates good decisions—

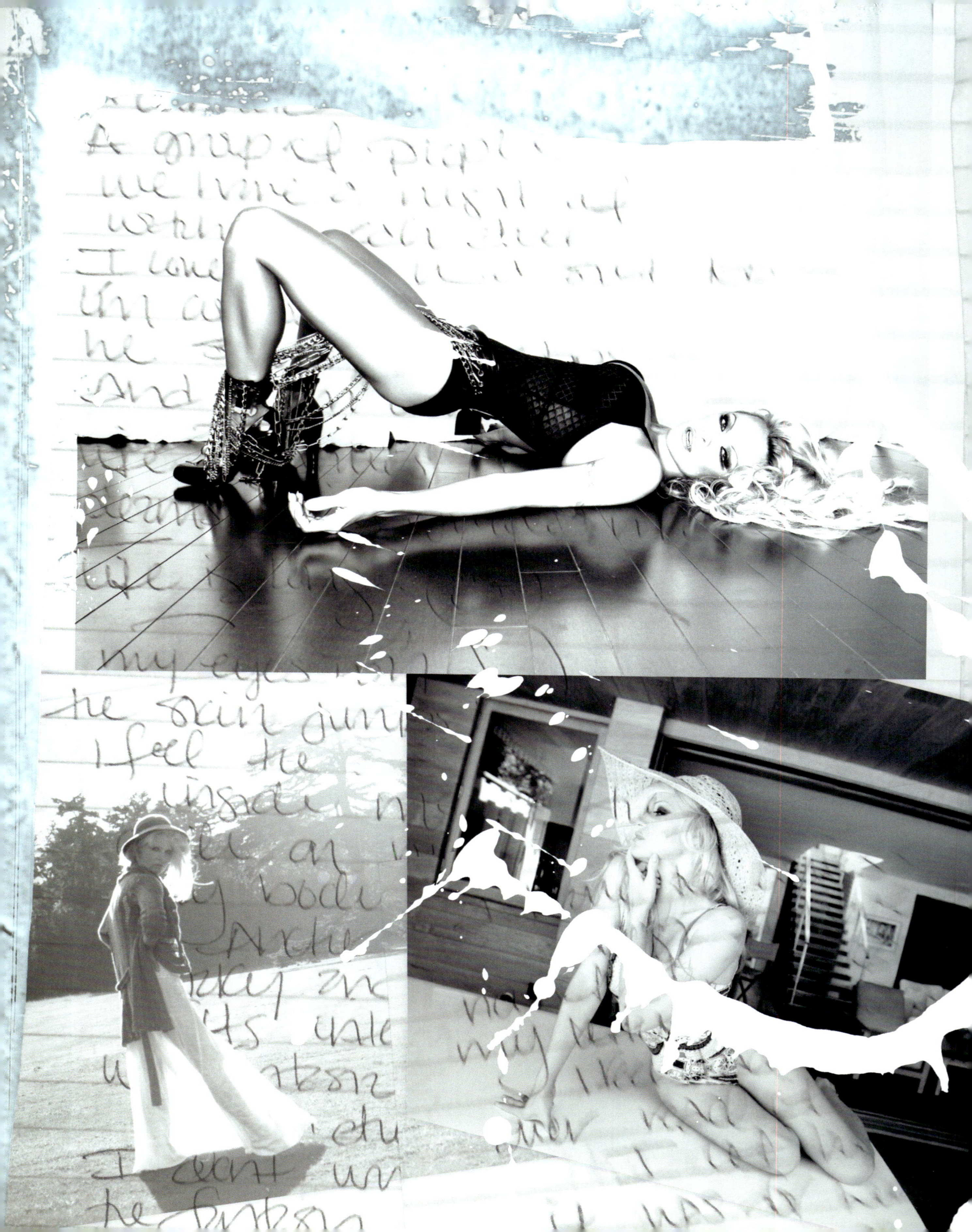

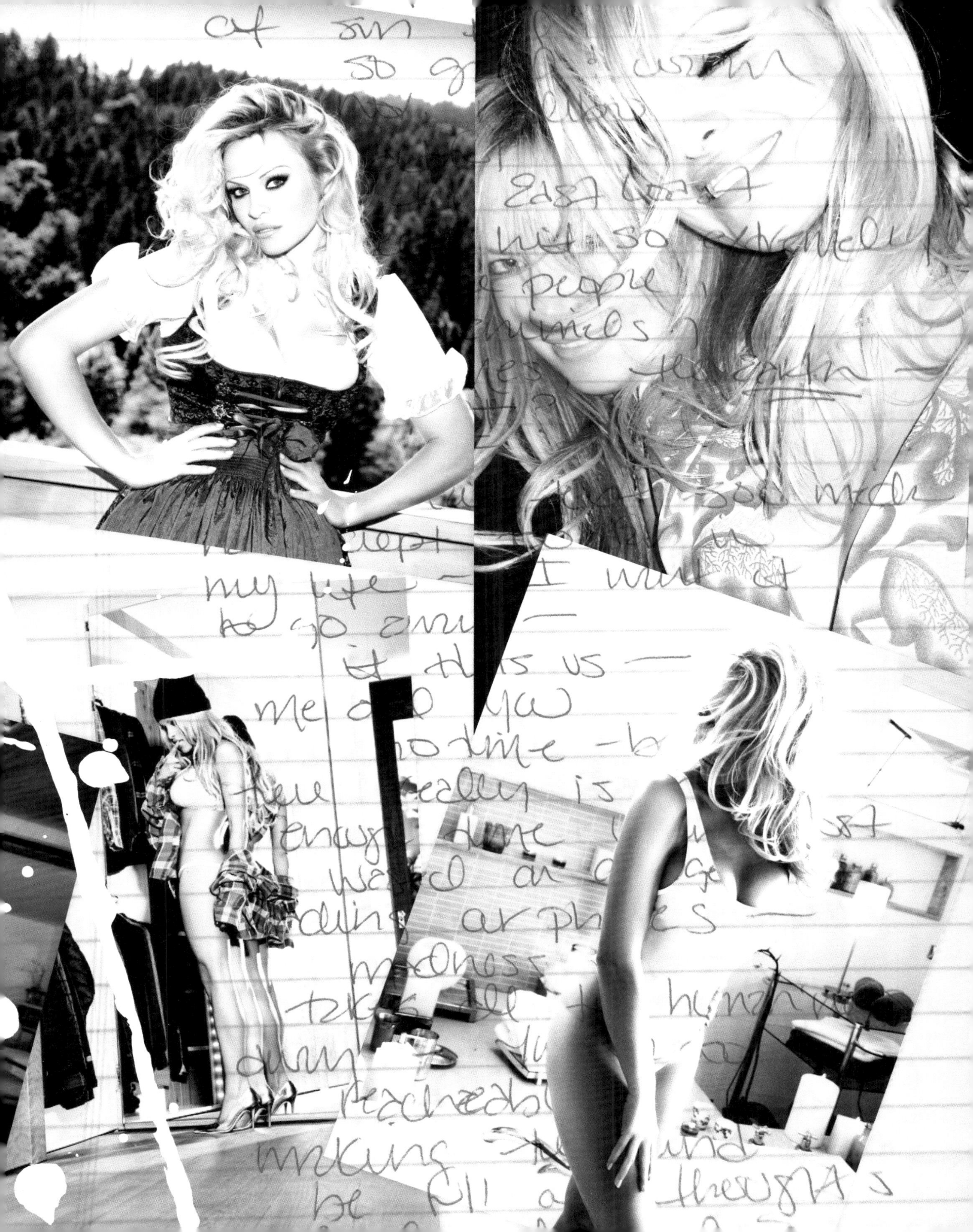
my life — I want
to go away —
it this is us —
me and you
there really is
enough time

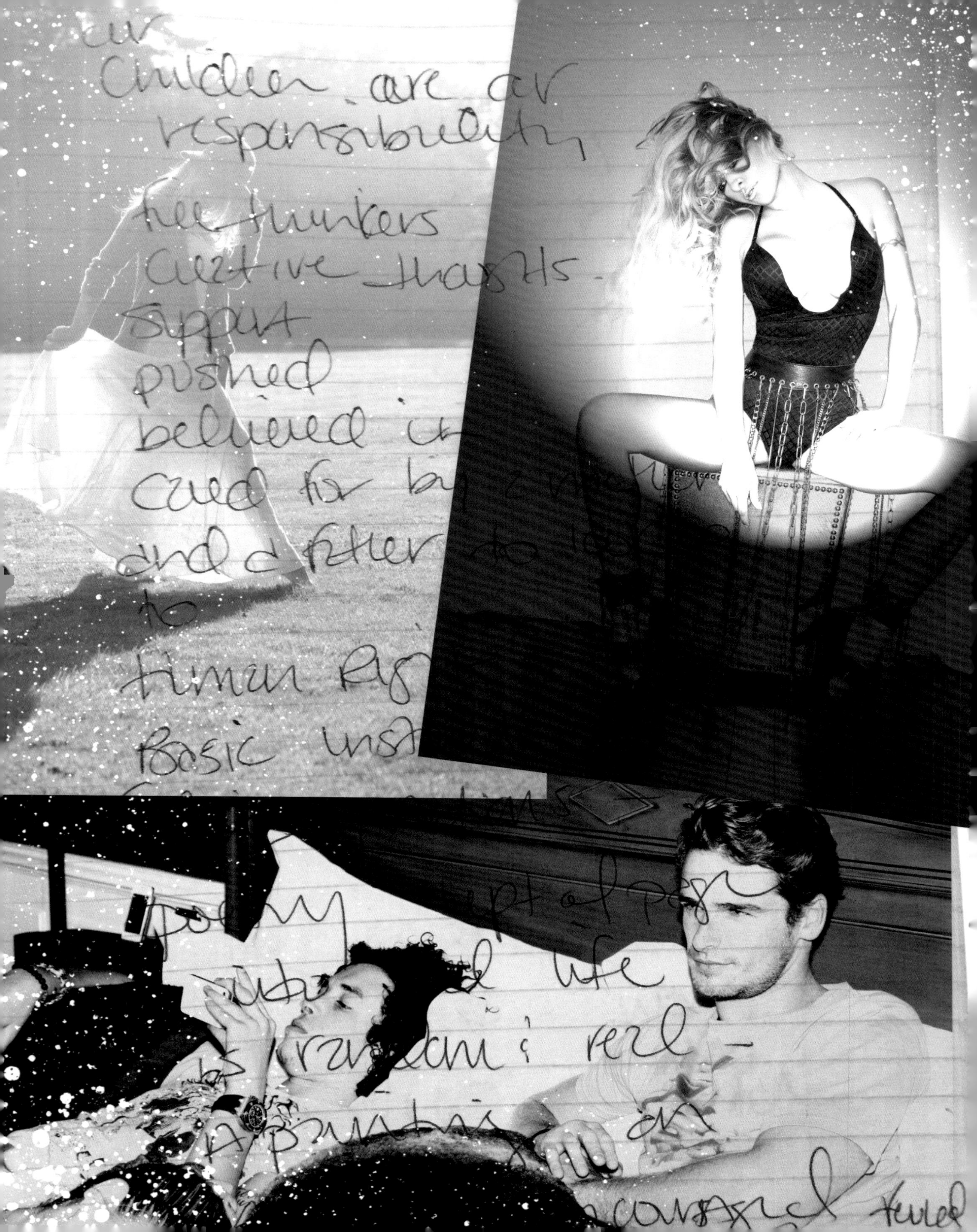

our
children are our
responsibility

free thinkers
creative thoughts
support
pushed
believed in
cared for
and father
to
human rig[hts]
basic inst[inct]

poetry
life
freedom is real

Blue Absinthe
Whistler white
Clarity of mind
Love is blind
My boys feel loved
My angels are here
Called me to come . . .
Snowflakes of thoughts
Spontaneously perfect
Different directions
Lost and found
Inspiring ground
Golden toes
Shiny eyes . . .
Searching, testing,
    pushing, feeling
No fear of heights
Challenge hovers
Love me tender
The dance, the spin, the
    dip, the walk
Tummy aches when I
    feel . . .
Intensity of right
Chocolate from Brandon
A sweet thought
A hungry man awaits
A loving wish to humanity
A sleeper

Not a gushing, explosion
    of what?
A misty colored memory
Heavy choices
A thought of truth . . .
A water want . . . a peel of
    brain . . .
A lie, guessing in the
    wind
Of where we go from
    here . . .
(Off course . . .
    compass in pack . . .
    found out . . . dirty
play . . .)
Ribs don't ache
Tears don't come
Love never lies

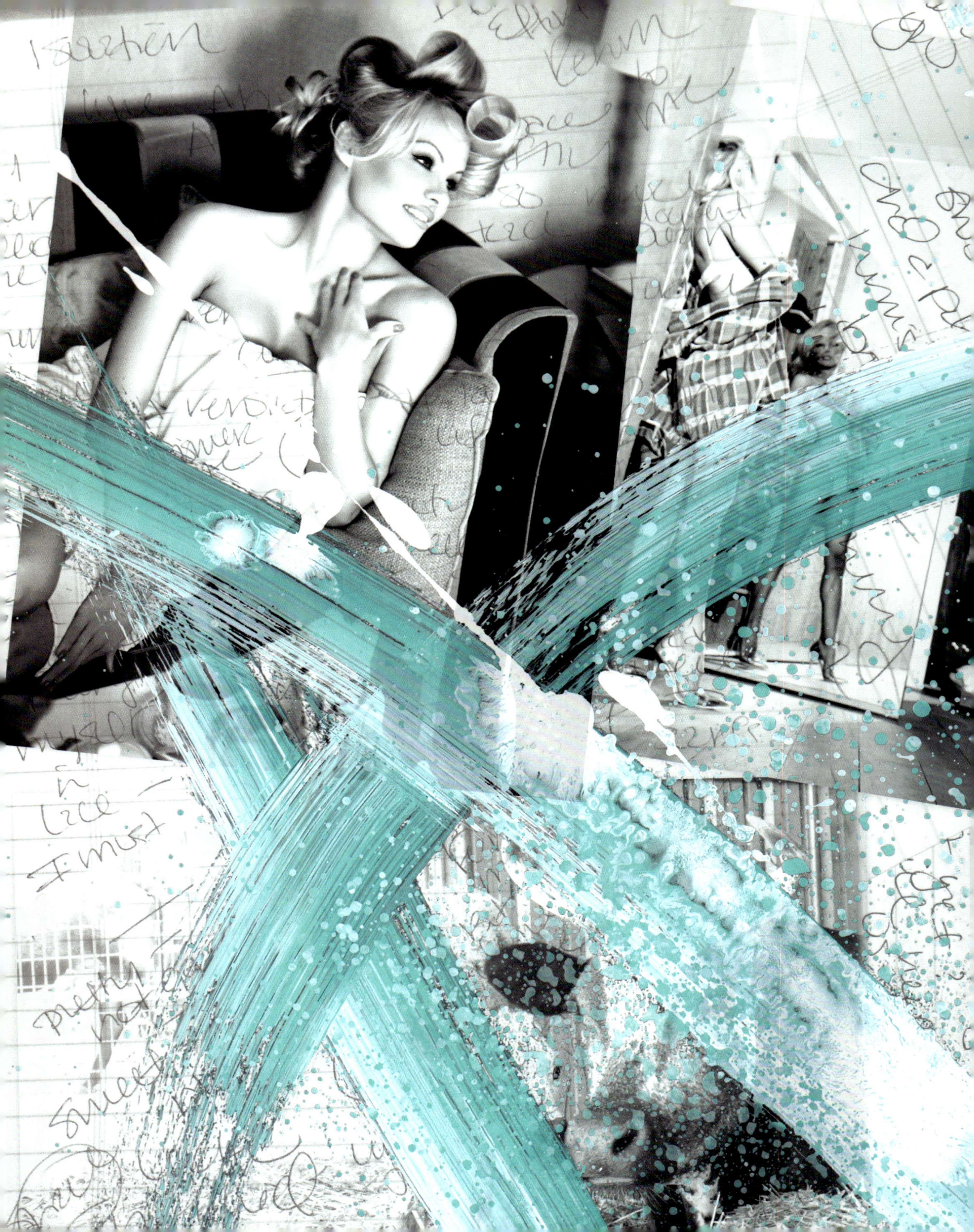

A creature braving her address in the open before your eyes — A magic tride, of worth & wonder

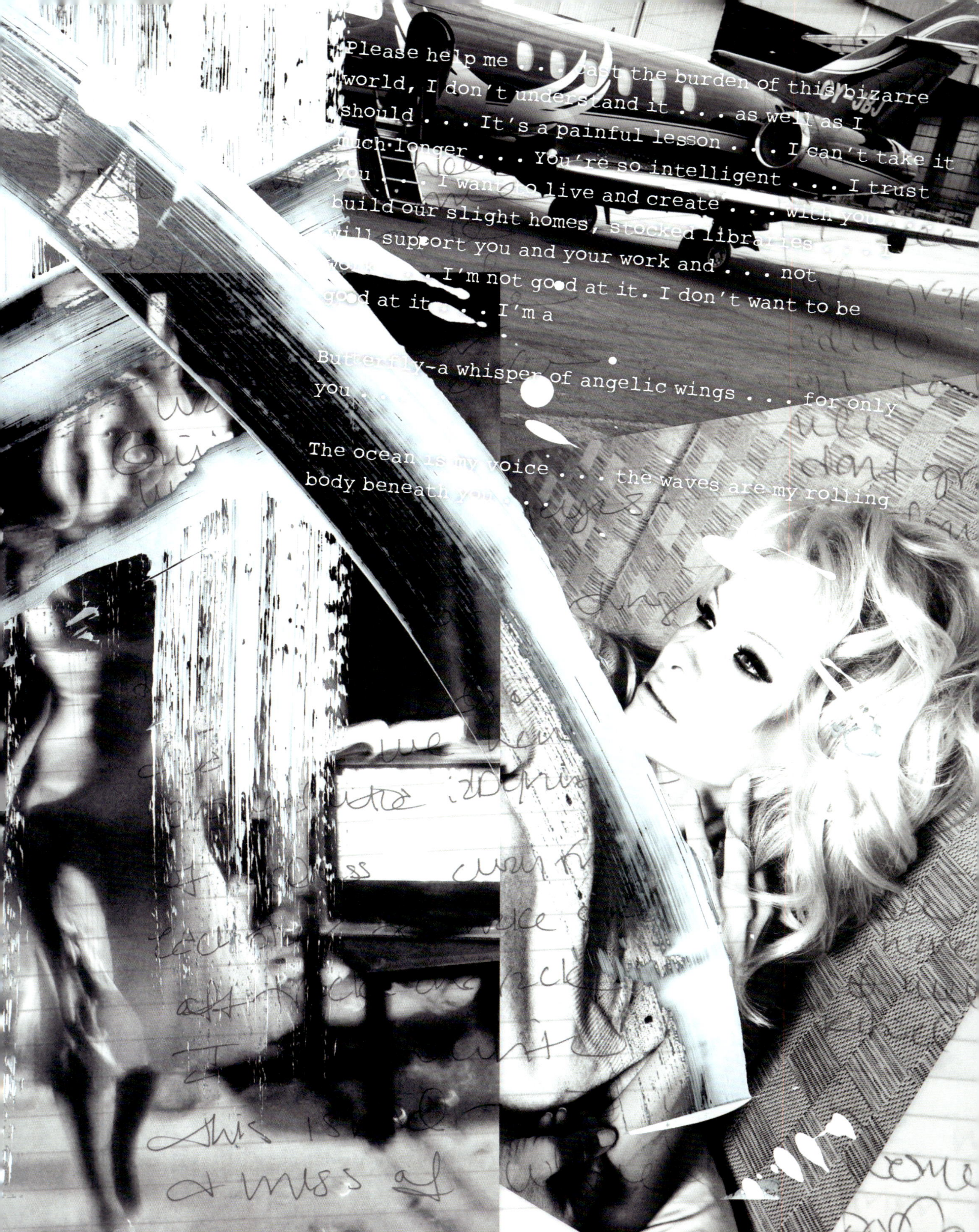

Please help me . . . . . . cast the burden of this bizarre world, I don't understand it . . . as well as I should . . . It's a painful lesson . . . I can't take it much longer . . . You're so intelligent . . . I trust you . . . I want to live and create . . . with you . . . build our slight homes, stocked libraries . . . will support you and your work and . . . not . . . I'm not good at it. I don't want to be good at it . . . I'm a

Butterfly—a whisper of angelic wings . . . for only you . . .

The ocean is my voice . . . the waves are my rolling body beneath your . . .

Project blue book/
red book
I do not believe in emasculating men-
We are all individuals growing at our
   own speed/pace.
Acceptance, with healthy boundaries-
   emotionally, physically,
sexually-I am not a feminist. I do
   think we have our archetypal
roles to play.
for good reasons.

Sexually leaves grey area.
-who is to judge what goes on between
   two consenting adults-(as
long as there is respect)
I think repression causes divorce. I
   am an advocate of marriage-
but-modern technology is making it
   even more difficult to be
monogamous-I prefer to be with one
   person-committed

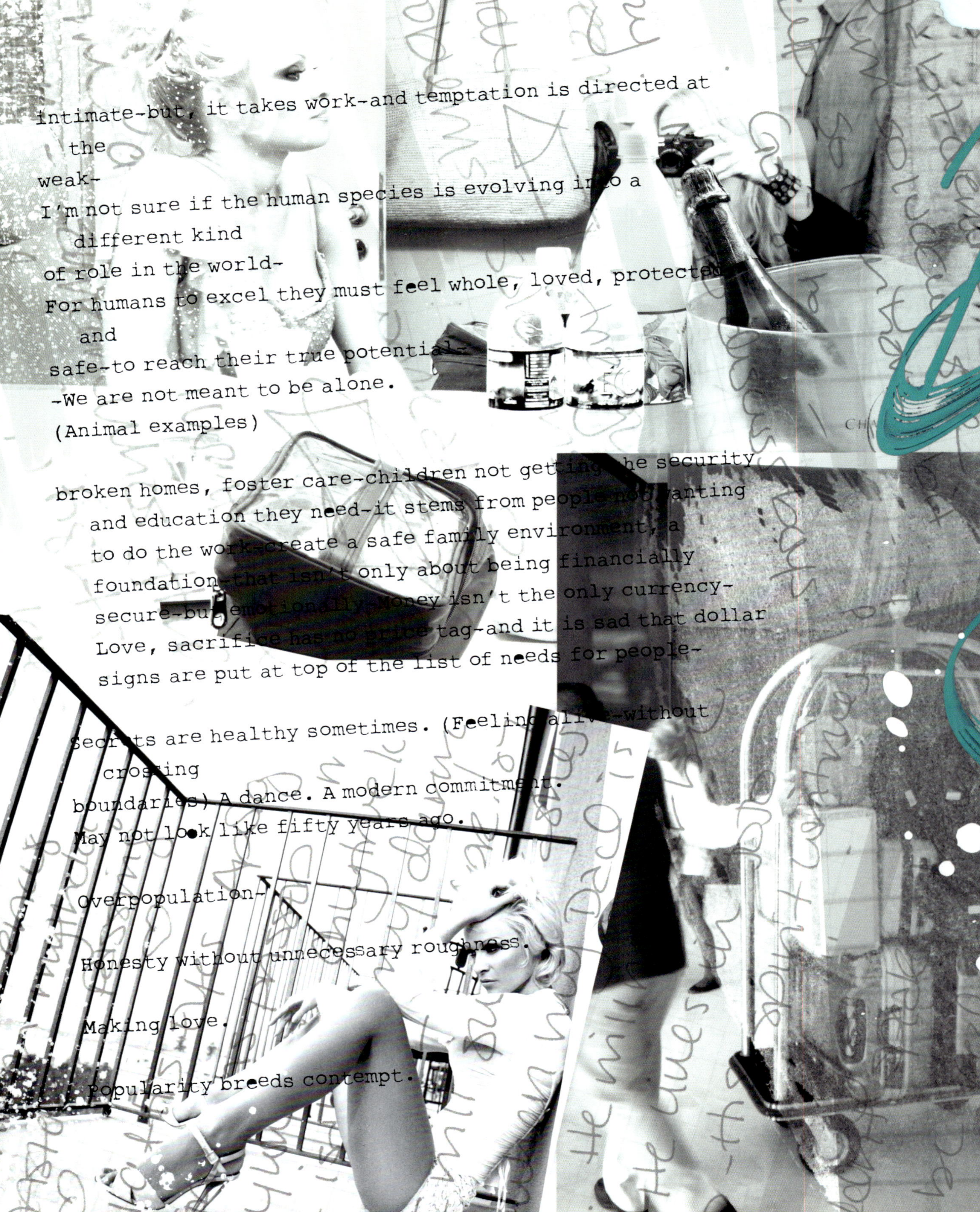

intimate-but, it takes work-and temptation is directed at
  the
weak-
I'm not sure if the human species is evolving into a
  different kind
of role in the world-
For humans to excel they must feel whole, loved, protected
  and
safe-to reach their true potential-
-We are not meant to be alone.
(Animal examples)

broken homes, foster care-children not getting the security
  and education they need-it stems from people not wanting
  to do the work-create a safe family environment, a
  foundation-that isn't only about being financially
  secure-but emotionally-Money isn't the only currency-
Love, sacrifice has no price tag-and it is sad that dollar
signs are put at top of the list of needs for people-

Secrets are healthy sometimes. (Feeling alive-without
  crossing
boundaries) A dance. A modern commitment.
May not look like fifty years ago.

Overpopulation-

Honesty without unnecessary roughness.

Making love.

Popularity breeds contempt.

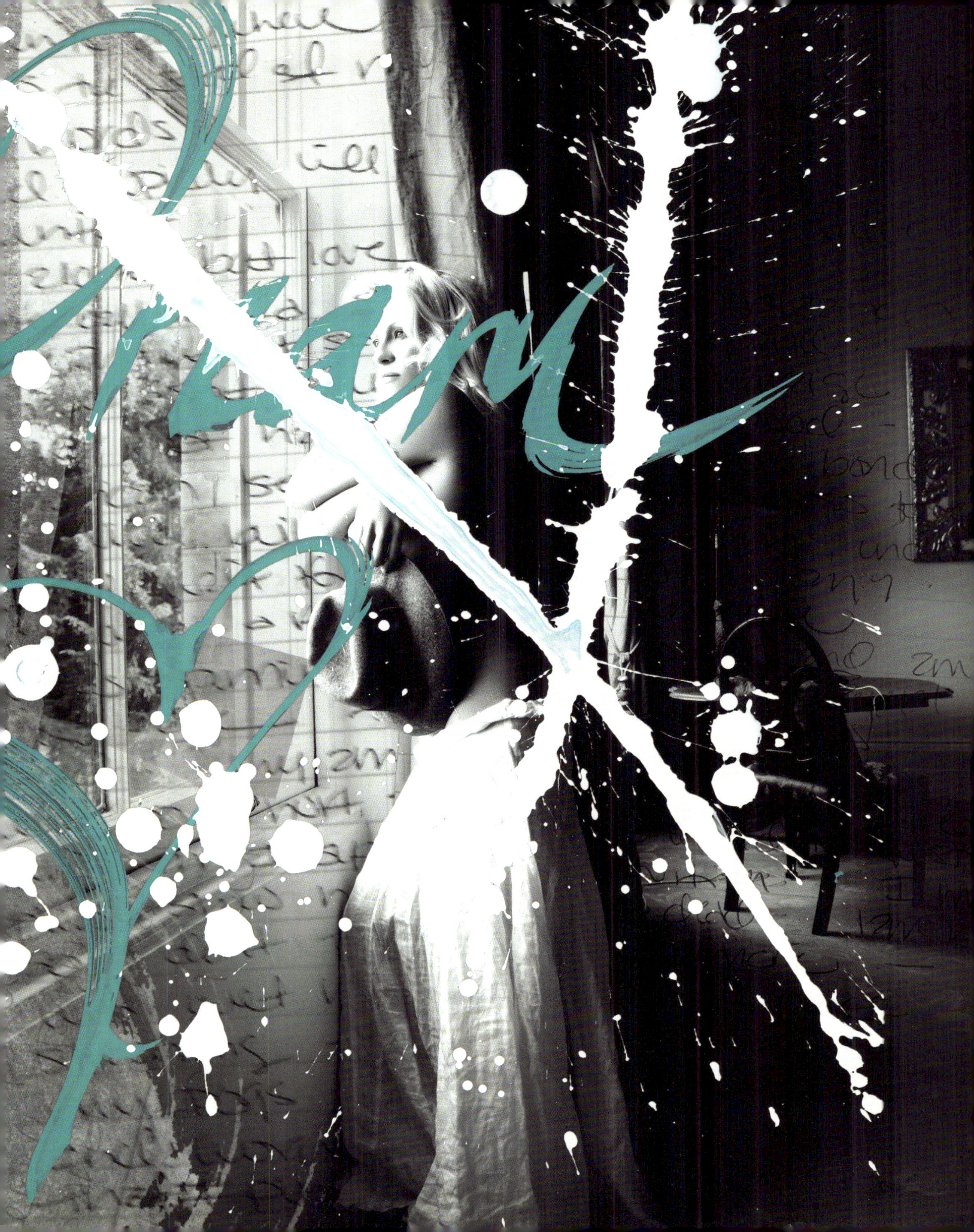

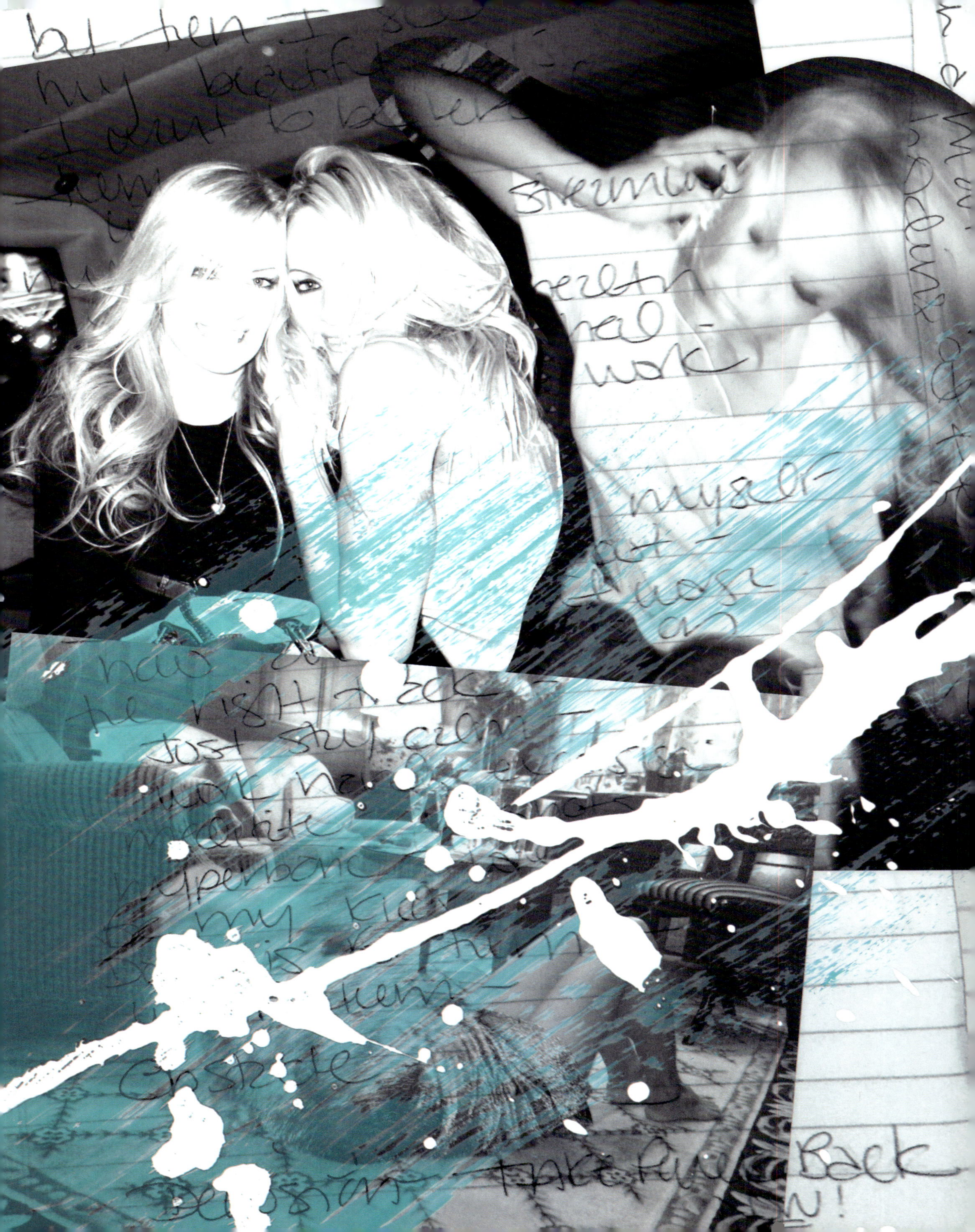

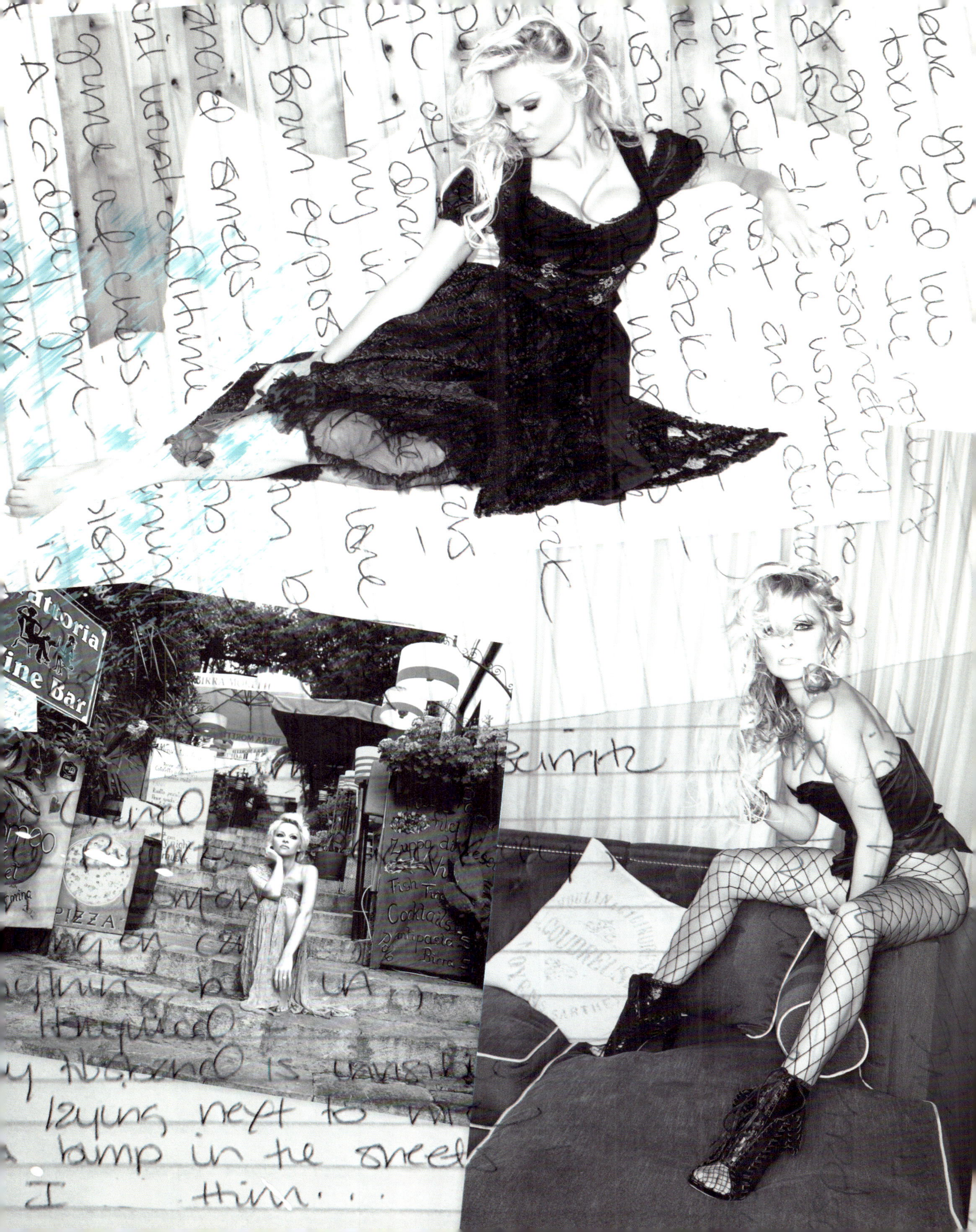

From the wild shores of Taormina, Italy—under Mt Etna, blown its top—I couldn't sleep—energized—

An impromptu shoot at 5am—makeup from night before—I poured into my lavender Vintage Gianni Versace gown...draped over the drum kit in the lobby—I wondered, *Where have come from?* —the drums still bang in my head—

Emma Dunlavey and I thought—take off the shoes and run barefoot through the streets—if only we had champagne—but that was then...this is now...

Emma reminds me of a young Ellen von Unwerth—she has a sexy natural photographic style—we click effortlessly and laugh endlessly—I'm glad to call her my friend (for 20 years...)

Oh—and...we have photos—they tell a story or...too many...

Tempted—but we might wait on that one—might do a book, include some poetry—

I'm a scribbling—rambling—heated woman—rolling around in hotel rooms full of broken glass, rose petals—and a cast of characters—some

stay the same—my funny, creative friends every day is "Arts and Crafts"...lost many an eyeliner writing poems in the bathtub...till the words fell into the drain—

—while no one was awake yet, except a scruffy black cat (my lover), following us—even the paparazzi were asleep—it felt very "La Dolce Vita"—such a peacefulness in the morning—just an echoing giggle between two girls—and the meow of a horny stray—quite a contrast left over—while the vibrancy of the evening before still had my head spinning...local music, old people holding hands—so romantic—dancing in the streets—and I'm sure on checkered table tops—I didn't want to leave—but then remembered—I had a husband... and children....and I better get home—That's a whole other bag of worms—worth photographing—life is interesting, challenging—love is a vulnerable place. We all need to escape sometimes...

It makes us better wives—and moms...

My lover IS a black cat—harmless...symbolic—

tortured—

misunderstood...

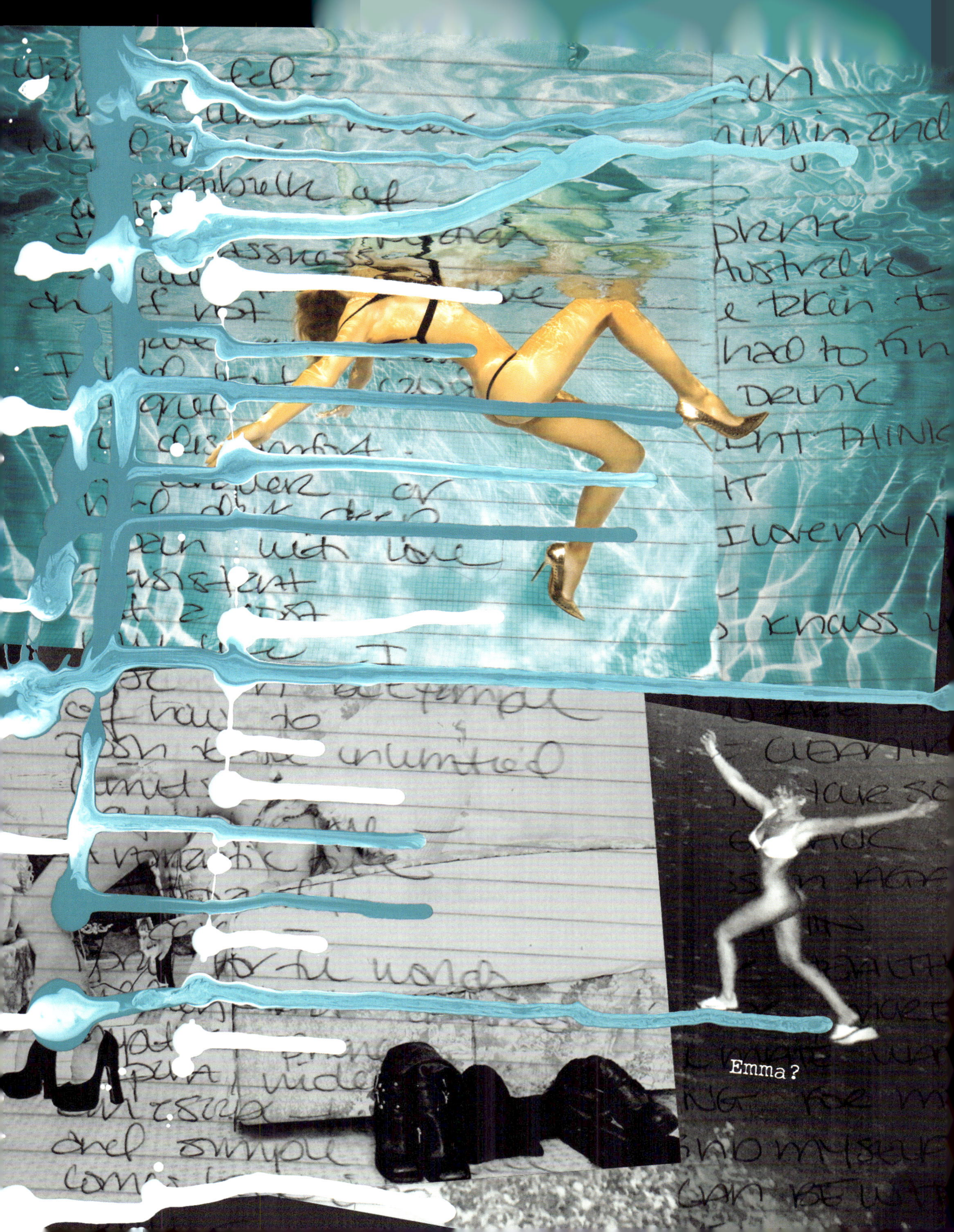
Emma?

with met
[illegible] and inconsistent
[illegible] sunsets shine
[illegible] miss

[illegible] ever my
[illegible] mischievous [illegible]
[illegible] of [illegible]
often around the fire [illegible]
[illegible] [illegible] the
strength and wisdom
no women can [illegible] eyes

whisper
not bad guy
[illegible]

[illegible] tongue

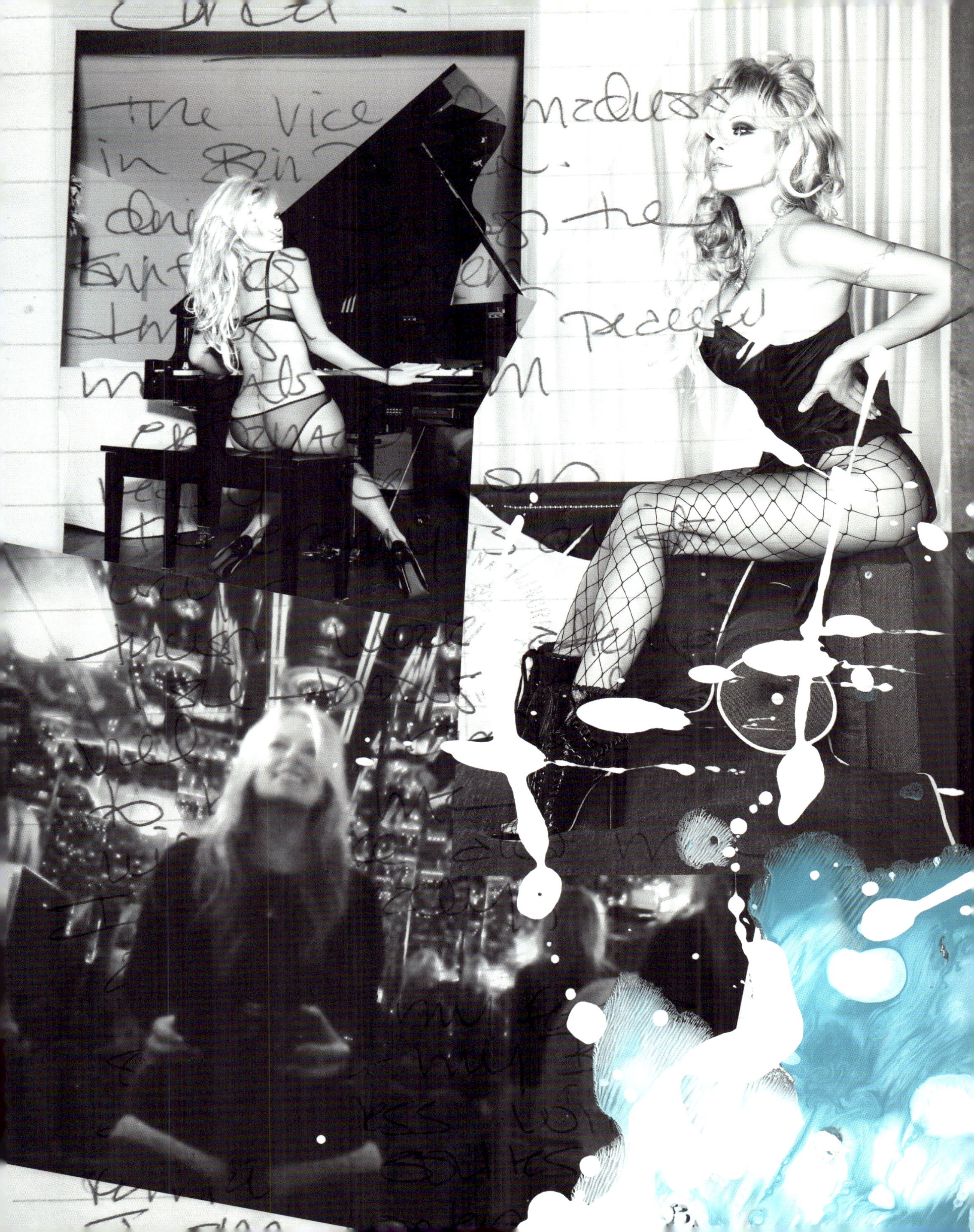

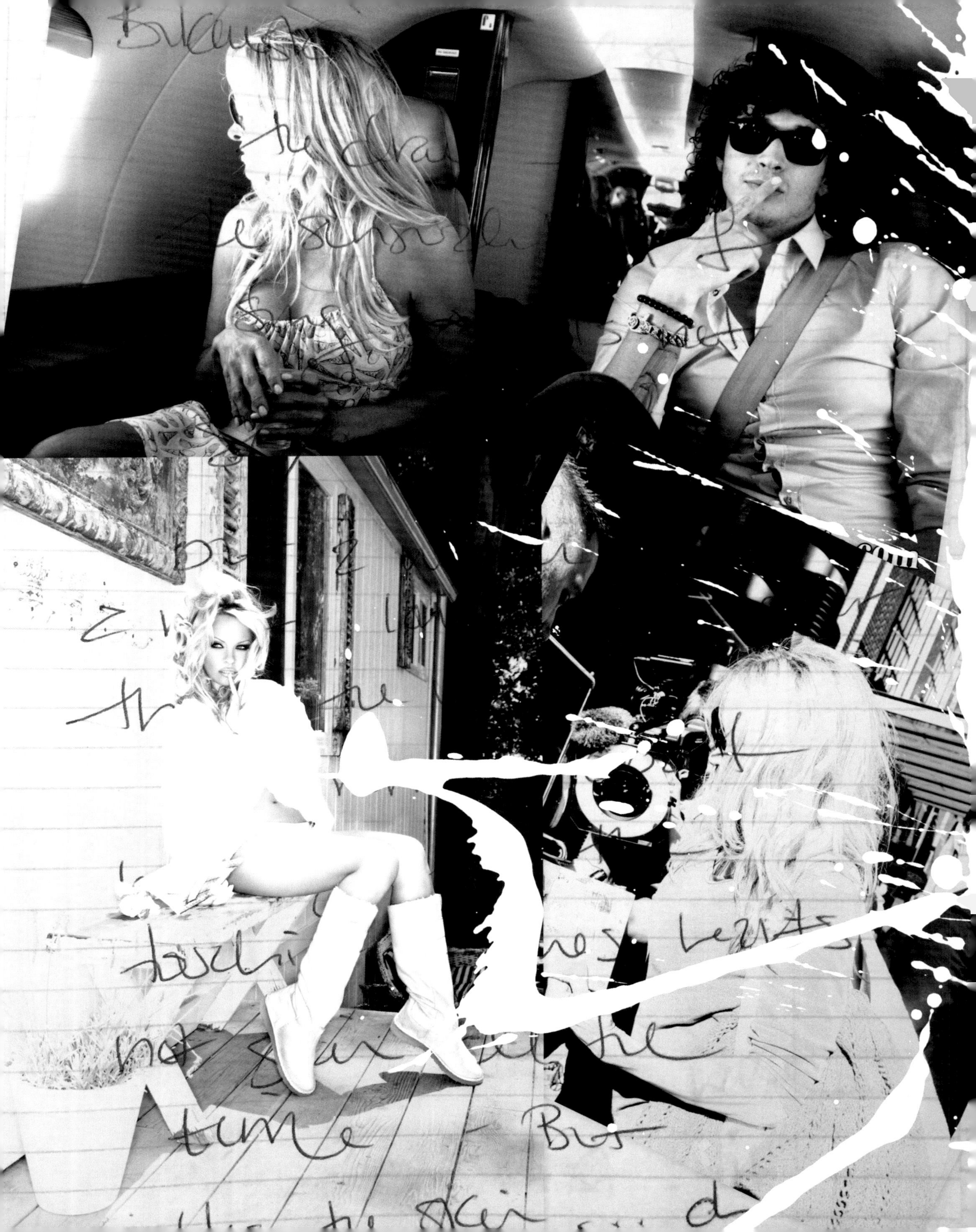

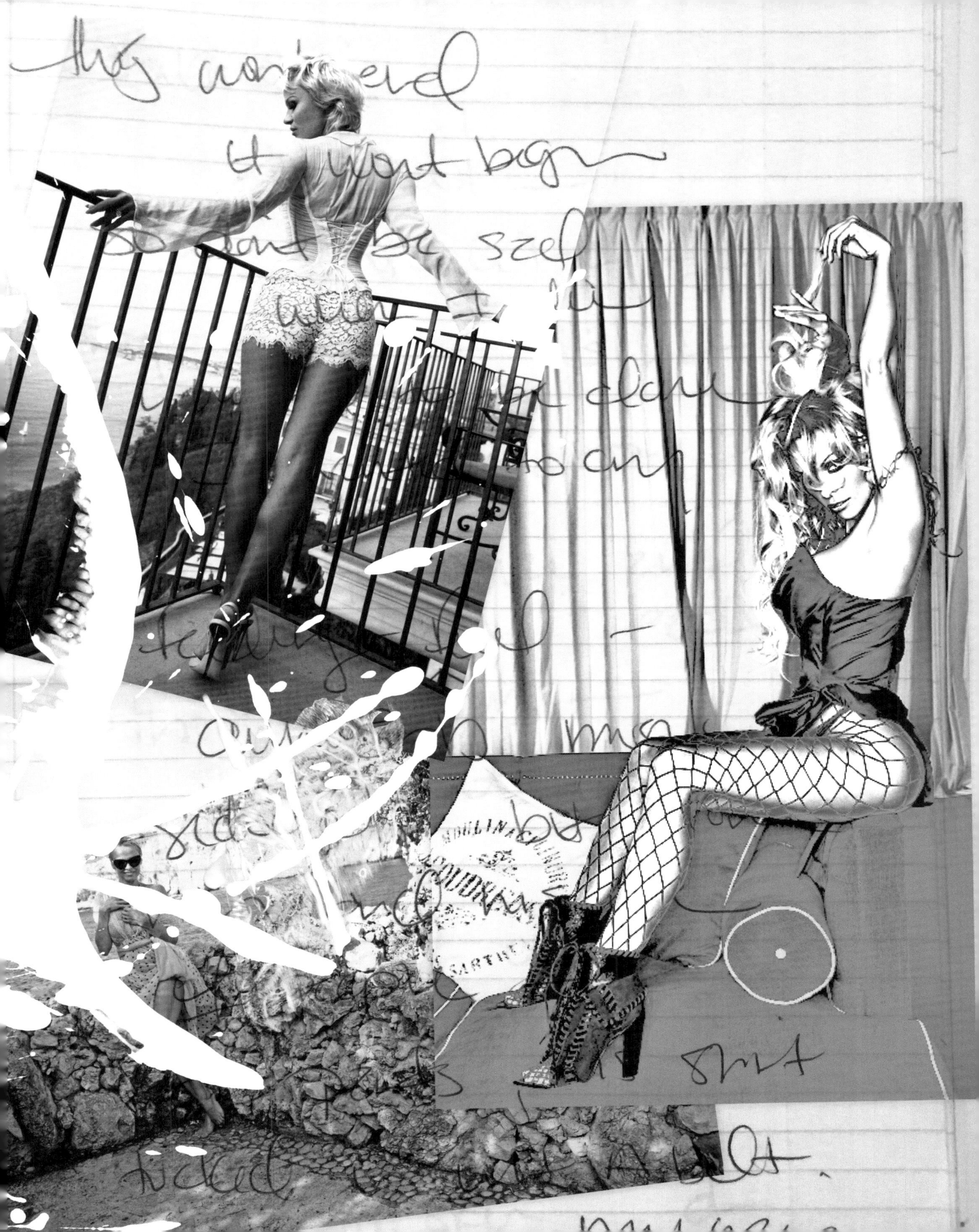

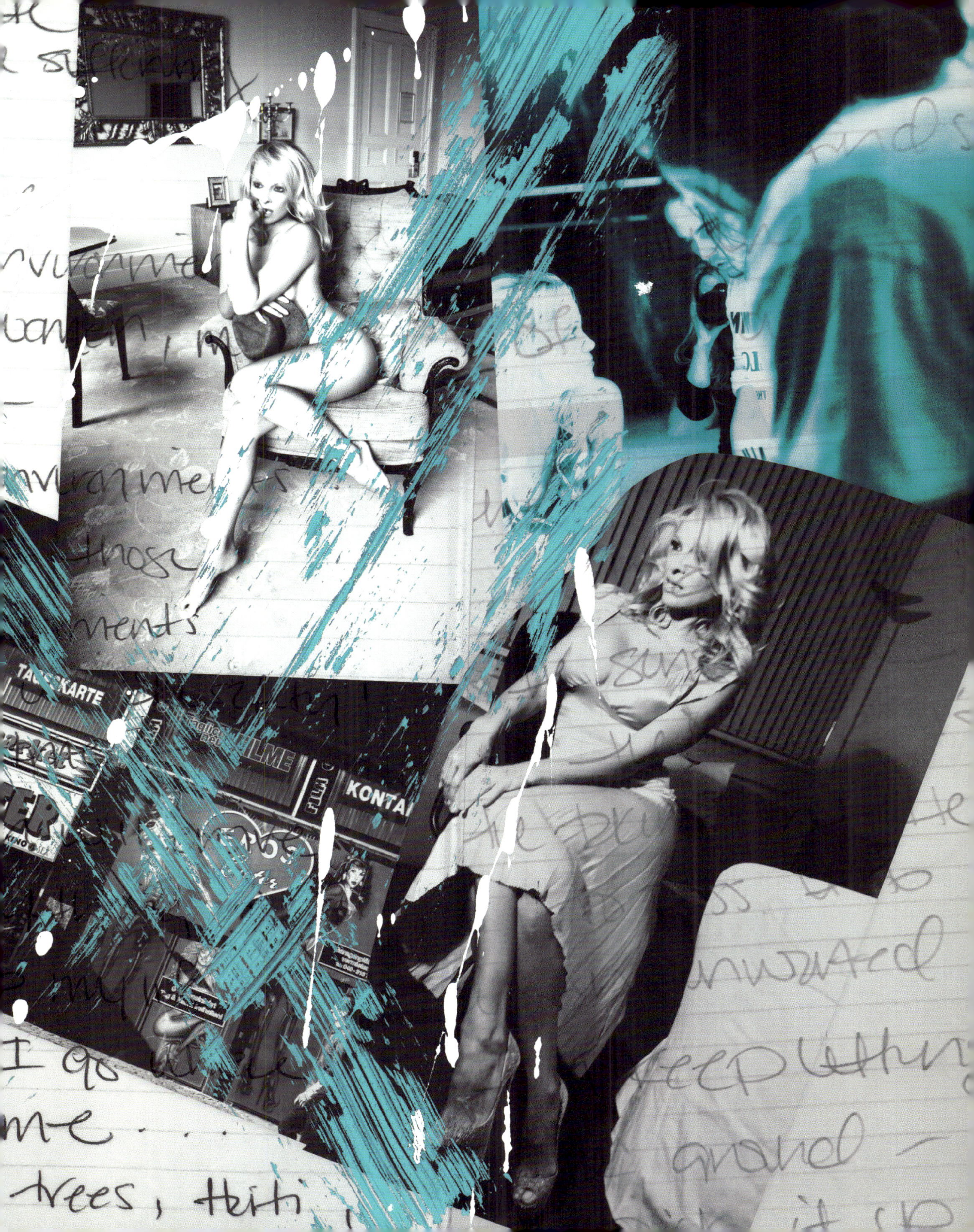
TAGESKARTE
LME
KONTA

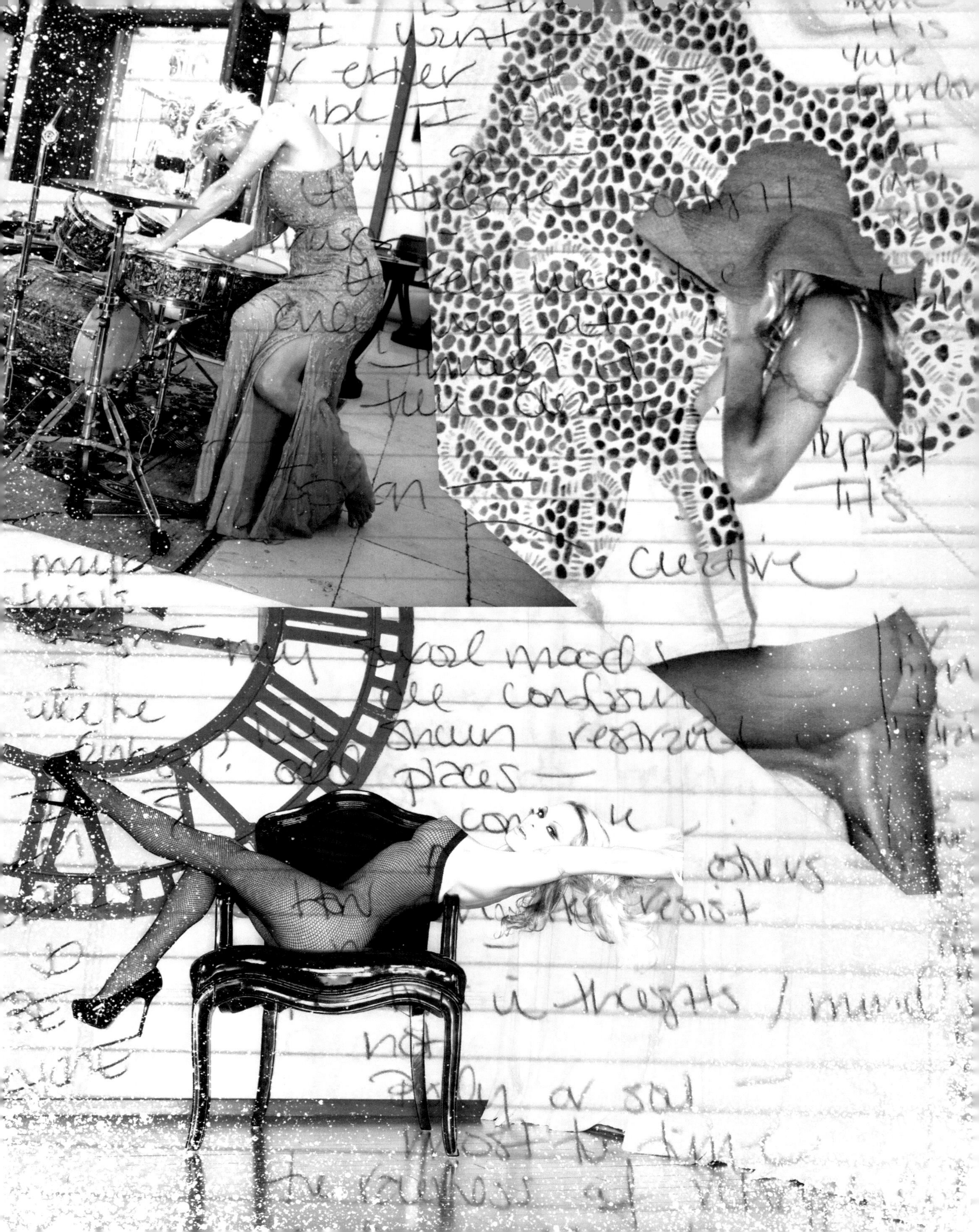

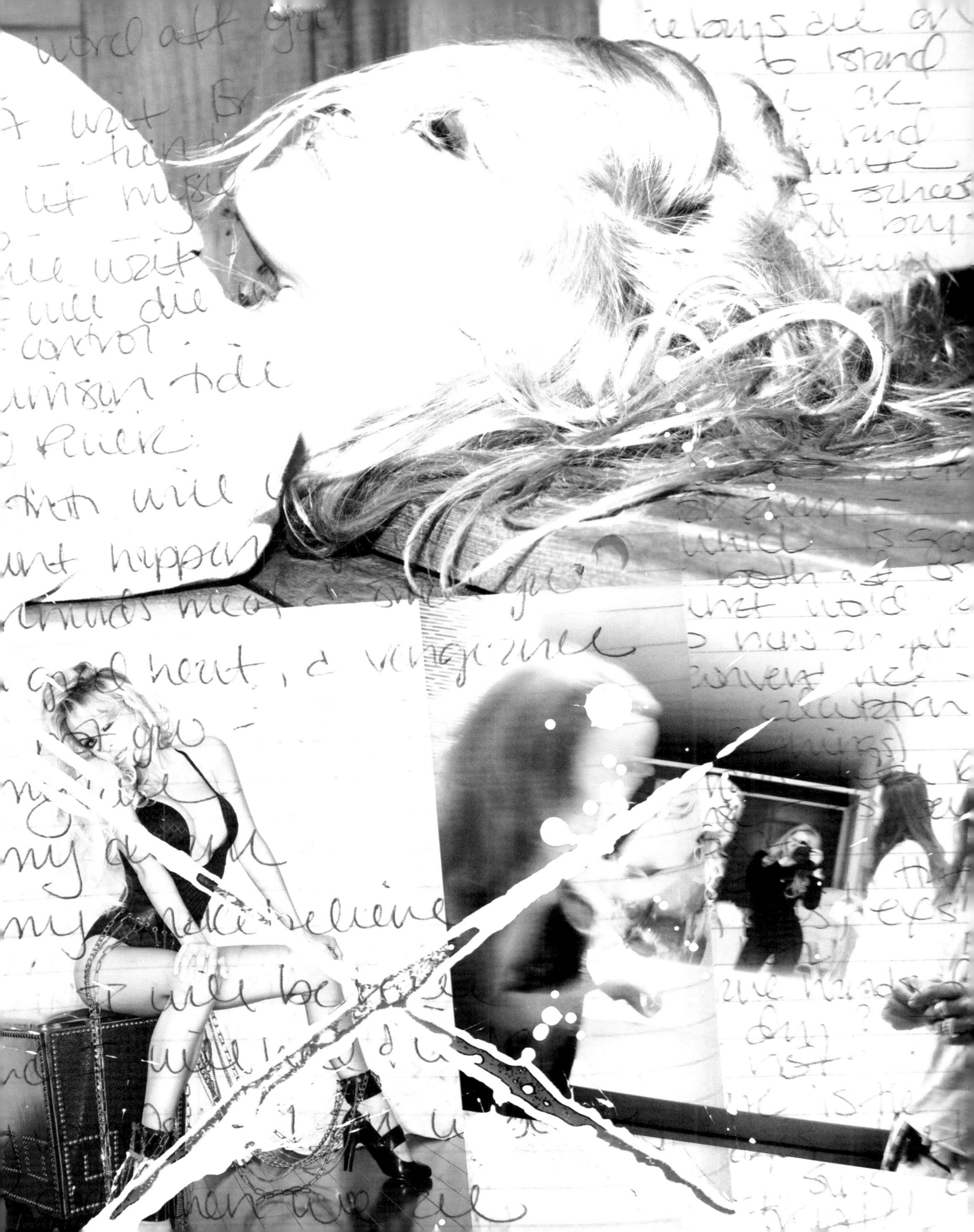

[illegible] word aft you [illegible]

I writ B [illegible]
— then h[illegible]
let mysl[illegible]
[illegible] writ
[illegible] will die
control.
[illegible]
unsun tide
[illegible]
Ruck.
then will y[illegible]
unt happen[illegible]
[illegible] meat [illegible]

[illegible] heart, a vengerice [illegible]
[illegible] you —
[illegible]
my [illegible]
my [illegible] believe [illegible]
I will be [illegible]
[illegible] will [illegible]
[illegible]

[right column, illegible handwritten fragments]

From your sea . . . to my shore
. . . The call of the siren . . .
Gallant you are . . .
Though I could swim . . . through
    sharky waters-
    I don't . . . a soft white
    billowy dress flies . . .
    dreamily, yet shrinks in the
    distance . . .
My handsome captain . . . His
    rest is due . . .
The dock has stood the test of
    time . . . clinging
    to it . . . this is where I grew
    . . . It has never let me down .
    . .
A sundial of the gods.
    Protections . . .
    Persephone . . . my dad meant
    to call me . . .
    . . . you know . . .
You are in the epicenter of hope-
    your brave soul, the only
    reality . . .
A force of nature . . . weeds . . .
    a rebel . . .
You have the power of a King, a
    cockiness
    of a cowboy . . . You're
    ruthless . . . Thank God . . .
    . . . in
The wild west . . . You hold a
    unique hand . . . a smoking gun
    . . . I'm just a girl . . . it's
    not my eyes, but my nose . . . .

. . . The hour glass . . . Sand
    slipping . . . just to be
    turned over and over again . . .
    . . . yes . . .
For now . . . in my travels, the
    sun sets on Bucharest-bath
    in the blood of young women .
London traipsing by Grace Kelly
    . . . Victoria and Albert .
    . I pull my hair back . . .
    see myself in the reflection
    of the glass in front of her
    tiara . . . her demure lovely
    clothes
Merlin laughs-King Arthur has
    all the answers . . . There is
    no why . . . I dream of holding
    soldiers . . . One
    nt to return to see . . . the
    room of Wolff, I wonder . . .
    small rocks rolling through
    my fingers . . . my pockets
    full . . . I want to live . . .
Or part of me . . . there are so
    many parts
Melancholy . . . I step one
    stiletto into Athens . . . the
    old
Acropolis glows in the moonlight
    . . .
Champagne trickles down my
    throat . . .

Lions . . . .
Time, space
alchemists we are
. . . gnawing . . . sweet
sadness . . .
Shivering—I'd helplessly
melt with arms
around me . . . But
no . . . it's better this
way . . . angry any way.
This doesn't flow. Too
many changes. Too many
ideas . . . Too much
technology . . . tap tap
tap . . . a mess . . .
While you drift . . .
I drift away . . .
When I'm home the baby king
fisher will . . . bring me
another fish . . . He's so
proud . . . it is the only
time I'm truly happy . . .
Some . . .
other places were not so
good but maybe we were
not so good when we were
in them . . .
Funny, I hold Hemmingway in
my hands . . .
Life is but a dream . . .

And this is just your small
memory of me . . .
A wildflower.
Imperfect.
I want to fix this rambling
. . . but . . . that just
ruins things . . .
I'll just send . . . before
it loses its depth . . .
Then you'll have a work in
progress, a capsule . . .
A make believe lover,
just add water . . .
Love is a child . . . raised
by wolves. There are no
bounds.
The blue whale is on her way
north . . .
I need to get out of the
way . . . the train rounds
the bend . . .
Breathless.
I jump.

Crazy girl, Px

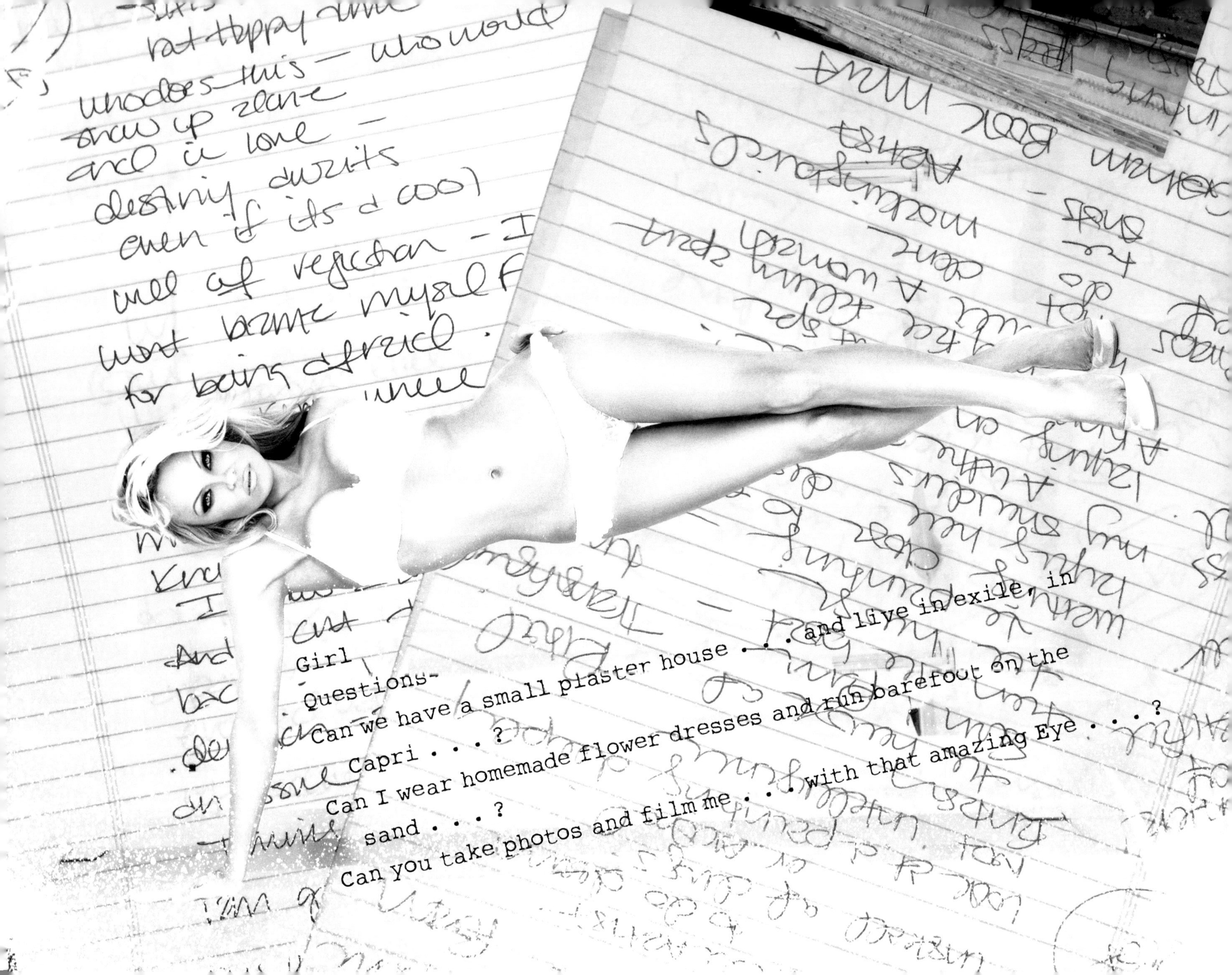

Girl

- Questions-

Can we have a small plaster house . . . . . . .and live in exile, in

Capri . . . ?

Can I wear homemade flower dresses and run barefoot on the

sand . . . ?   . . . with that amazing Eye . . . . ?

Can you take photos and film me . . .

...and can we write poetry and
listen to Jazz . . . just old
recordings?
...an we care for abandoned
animals-and have a garden of
...ldflowers, and herbs and
vegetables and . . .
...earn to speak Italian?
I'll better my schoolgi... ...re...
my cooking . . . I want to cook
f... our garden . . . bake bread
and make chocolate...
As you travel around the world
and work . . . no phones . . . we
write
letters-handwritten... ...
photos . . . music boxes . . .
thoughtful
gestures-crystal turtles . . .
always by post-
chocolates sustain me-until your
return
We'll have a tiny vineyard of
gypsies and fireflies
on bicycles . . . a Vespa
a painted boat . . .
I'll paint birds and words on the
walls . . . in turquoise

I will keep the house beautiful
for your return,-you bring me
sweet gifts, you surprise me
every time you come . . . I
never know
exactly when but feel you... be
home soon . . . with

a pearl, you've found in the
sea . . . or a flower, you've
chosen for me
...hair . . . or a tapestry of flowers
made by a monk . . .
In desperate need of his words,
his creativity, his piercing
blue
eyes . . . take me away, and
gain a glimpse of something to
...morously, lovingly
forever . . . grow
. . . sweetly provoke
...ursue,
...and feel complimented
...fueled
a gentle morning breeze . . . a
tumescent glow . . .

a soft silk slip . . . 2 small
cups of strong coffee . . . wild
sleepy
blonde hair . . . smoky eyes . . .
catching off guard . . .
that little boy look . . . but an
undeniable man . . . a tiny
arched back
for your strong hand . . . A tango

A match of hearts and souls . . .
Cat and Mouse . . . I will teach
you
how to love me . . . You will look
after me, protect me, cherish
us, my

boys . . . they will look up to you . . .
You will be who they aspire to be
And that will make me love you
more . . . please
take my breath, . . . my feminine
life . . . just a woman . . . soft . . .
please help me cast the burden of this
bizarre world. I don't
understand it . . . as well as I should
. . It is a painful lesson . . . I
can't take it much longer-You're so
intelligent . . . I trust you . . . I
want to live and create with you-and
without you I know I'll
keep making the same mistakes . . .
I want to build homes together-stock
our libraries of books and art . . .
I will support you and your working-not
work-I'm not good at
it-I don't know if I want to be good at
it-I'm a
butterfly-a whisper of Angelic
wings . . . for only you
The ocean is my voice . . . the waves
are my rolling body beneath you-
but you . . .
your hair comforts me . . . rivers of
smoky wisdom . . .
In me you'll always sense . . . the

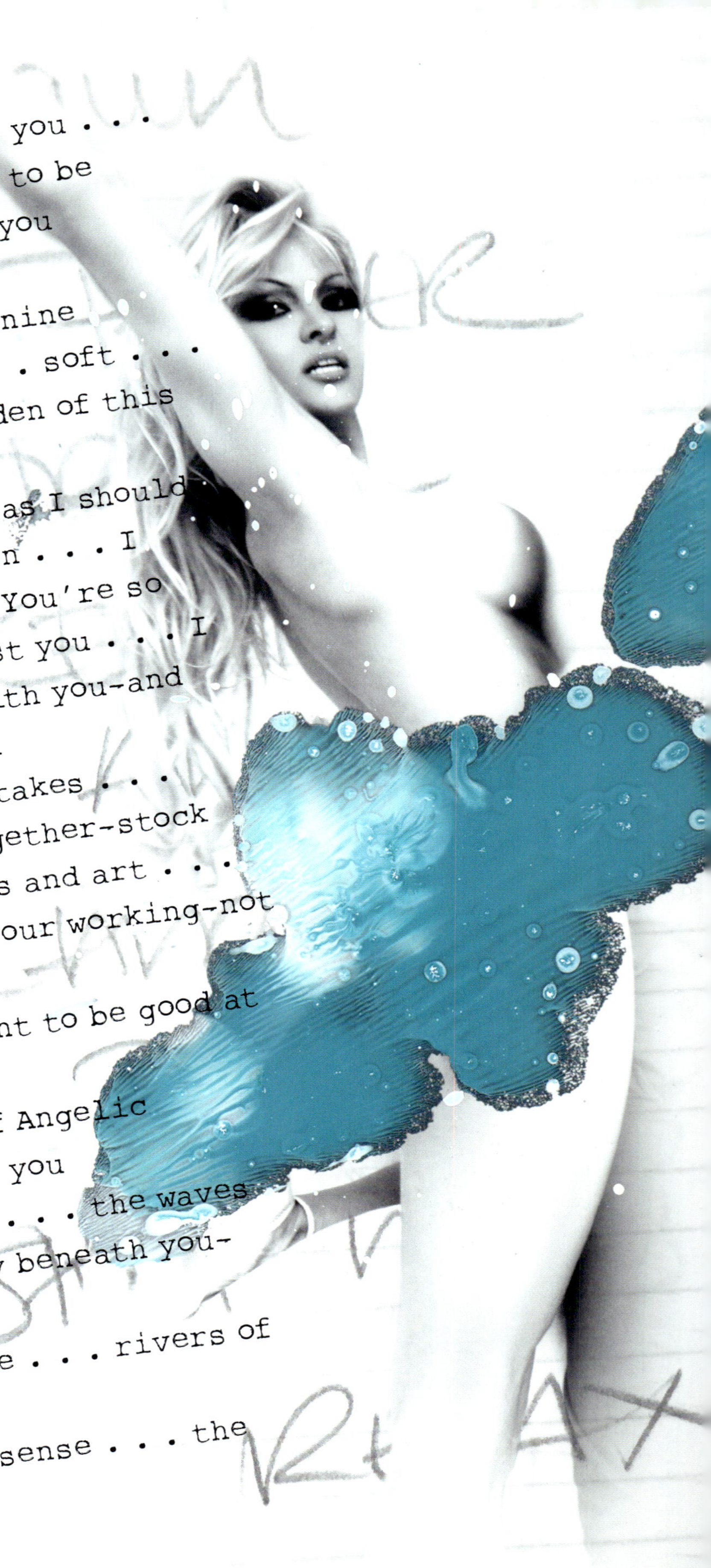

playfulness of
an aromatic garden of ocean lilies . . . I paint the sky
wild with
frozen pearls-a liquid brush . . .
Make love to me on a . . . lilac island of white . . .
pink and sandy
lavender's moon dripping of honey

I reach for you . . . but you're not there-I keep
reaching, tracing your body in my mind, lightly
pull on your heart strings-a lute-a hair, an eyelet
blouse . . . a
sheer draped skirt . . . a ring of gold-on my little toe

please take me . . . not to where I've been-
photograph pleasure, a tease . . . never stung . . . but
have bees . . .
as in Burgundy, the earth shall rock us to sleep . . .

let me be innocent for you-

I will learn to harness this curious fire in me-this is
all I want-
Put me here in my dream . . . and I'll be yours
forever . . . I await
your sweet return

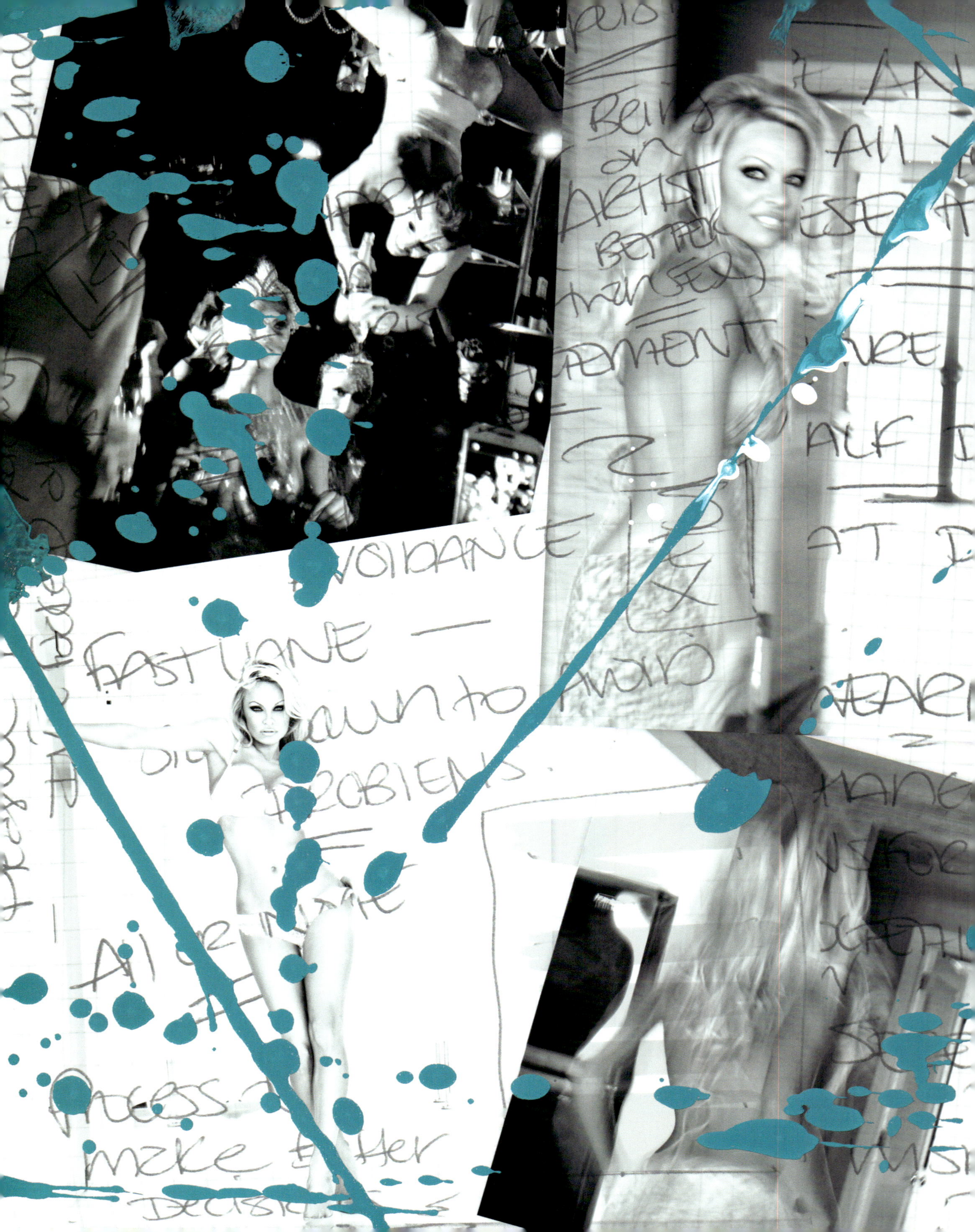
Being an ARTIST BETTER than sex
MOVEMENT
AVOIDANCE
FAST LANE —
own to avoid
PROBLEMS.
All or none
access
make better
decisions

I know you so well . . . the
harsh truths, the good,
the bad, the
ugly . . . there is no why . . .
only truth, graveness,
fairness for all,

trust, believe . . . me
You are a master . . .
worshipped
It won't end . . . because it
never began . . . it is-

I view you through a stained
glass window
fearless, humanity, tolerance
real kindness

A walk through town holding
hands . . . a festival . . .
street
performers . . .
fire eaters . . .
A glorious simply, colorfully
inspired, never ending sexy
meaningful life

I'm not perfect . . . I'm
insatiable . . . But-no Man
does this to me-in
the same way you drive me . . .
I can come and go . . . I'm up,
I'm down . . . and I always
hear how

happy you are . . . I drink a
little, then listen
more . . . of how bad you'd
be for me . . . Deaf does not
fall on champagne
ears . . . I believe you are
the one . . .
Fields of lavender await-I
can't take too many more
falls-My
heart awaits . . . save me from
myself
I will hold this image forever
I'm willing to be alone now-

You'll see
poor example so far. I know-
Or.
I'll end up in a cobblestone
perfumerie in Grasse, sad
about you
always-writing poems with
tears . . . making potions
to lure the man
I love-Quelle que Fleur?

. . . with the gravity of a mad
scientist-just might be the
only way
to survive, Px

REMBRANDT
MONET   RENOIR

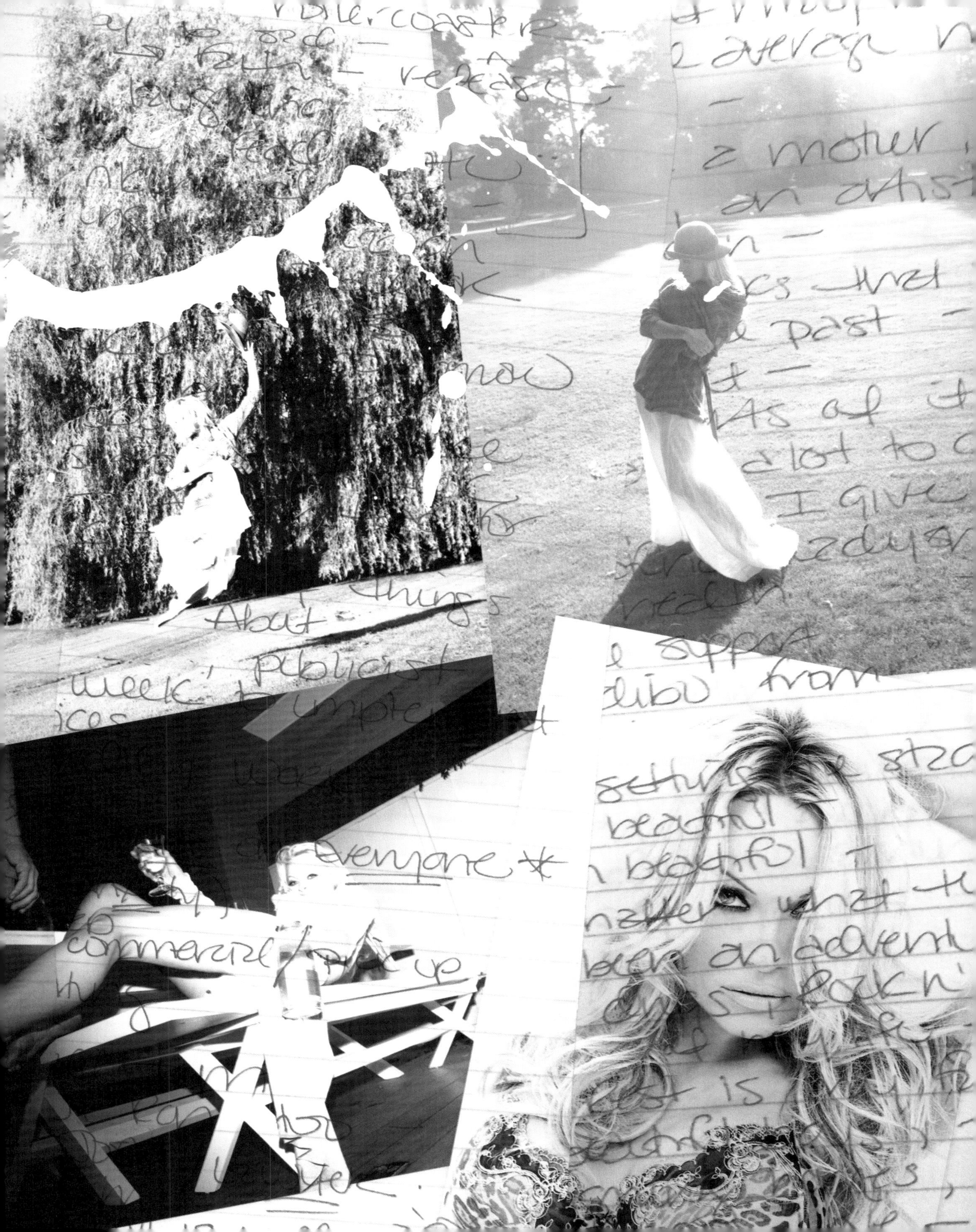

A journey inside the center of
my lusty soul.
The heat sends my mind wild.
Abandon all hope of fantastic dreams—
it is expanding whole
drops of champagne trickle
slipping sweetly down my throat.
I could swallow the sea in front of me.
A vortex of wet dreams.
A slow burn—
A red hot spanking—
A golden paddle—

submission-
Twisted-with fantasy-
Ibiza makes me hot-
so far.
Can Soliel Soleil.

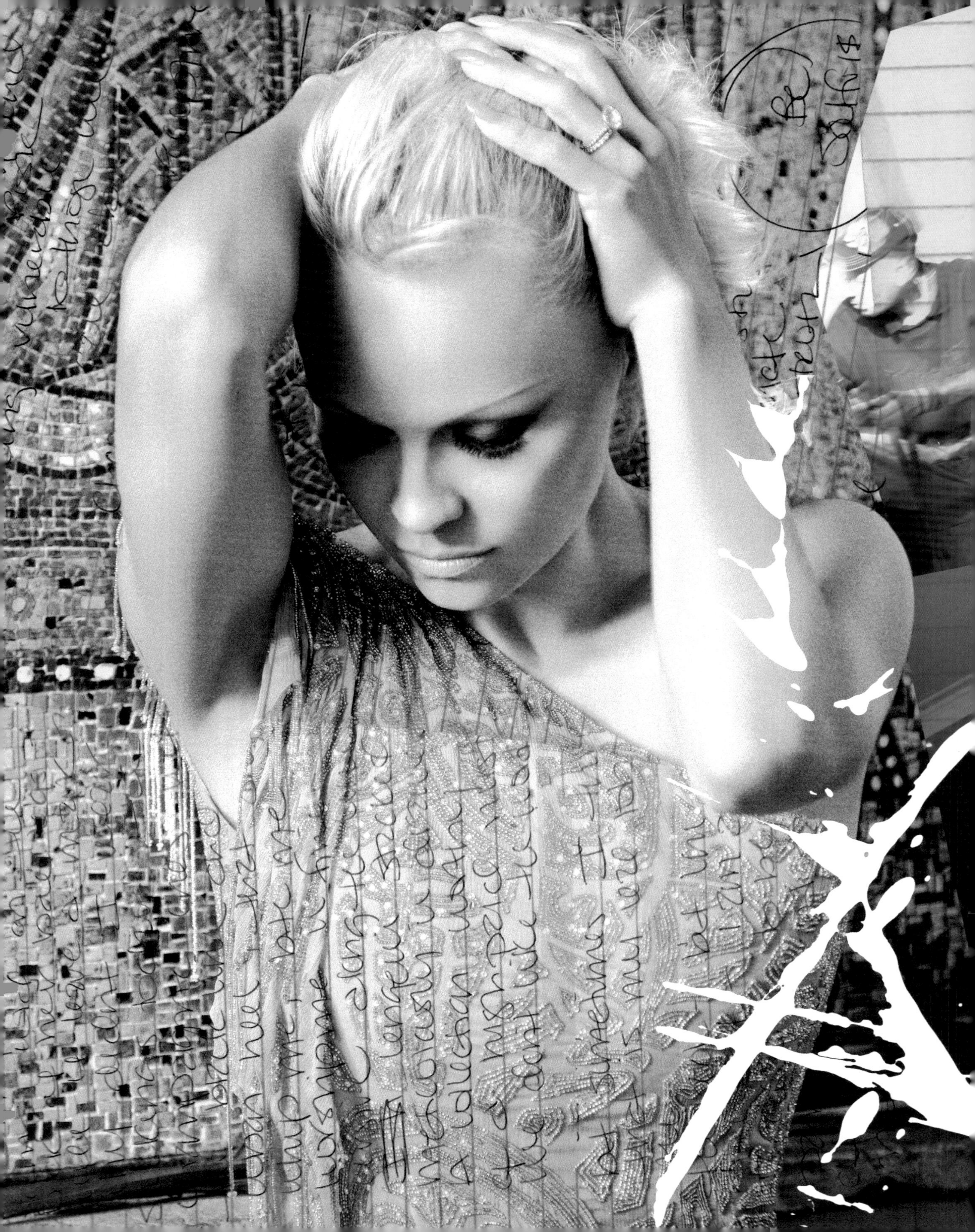

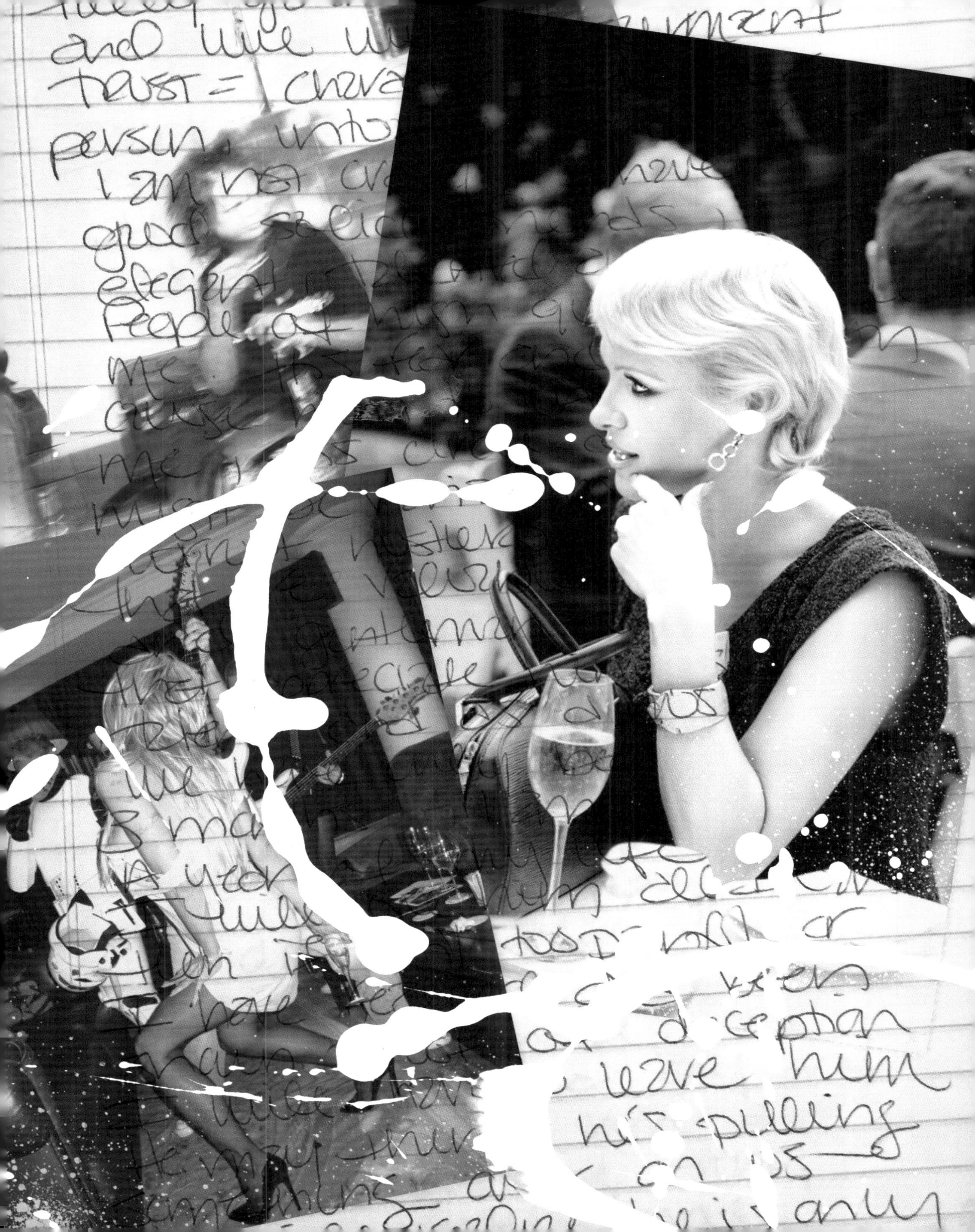

and like when
trust = chara
person, who
I am not cr
great social
elegant
people at
me

gentleman
appreciate
like
is ma
year

too I will or
even
deception
leave him
his pulling

...have happy
moments —
maybe 1/4 of my
time is happy —
I really am in love
with this enigmatic
man — but love to...
so clearly I don't...
to take his time
from what I love
this force to be —
He writes
letters —
teasing tenu...

I almost fun...
We drink too...
days are...
fun that my
sometimes —

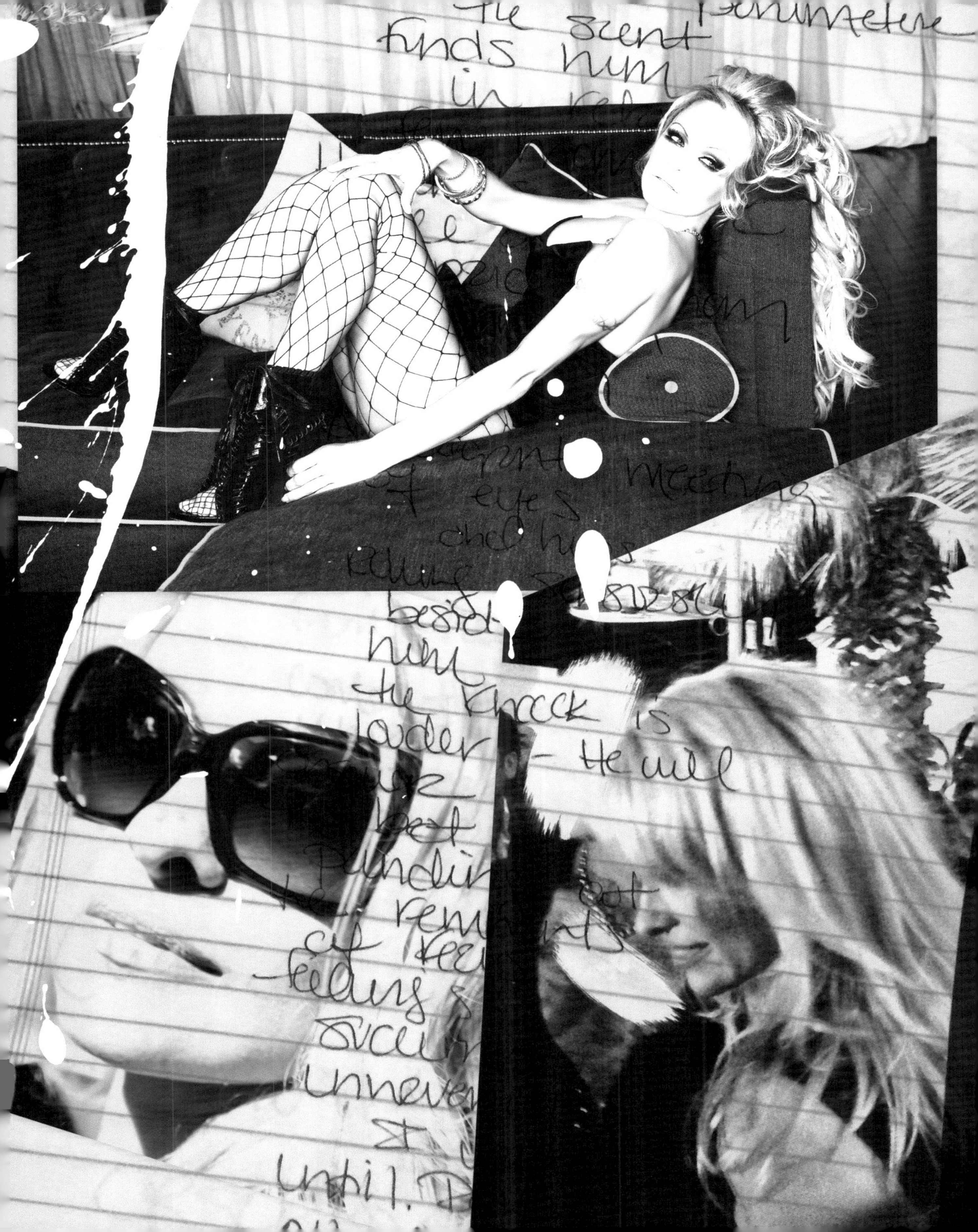

the scent
finds him
besides
him
the knock is
louder — he will
feelings
until

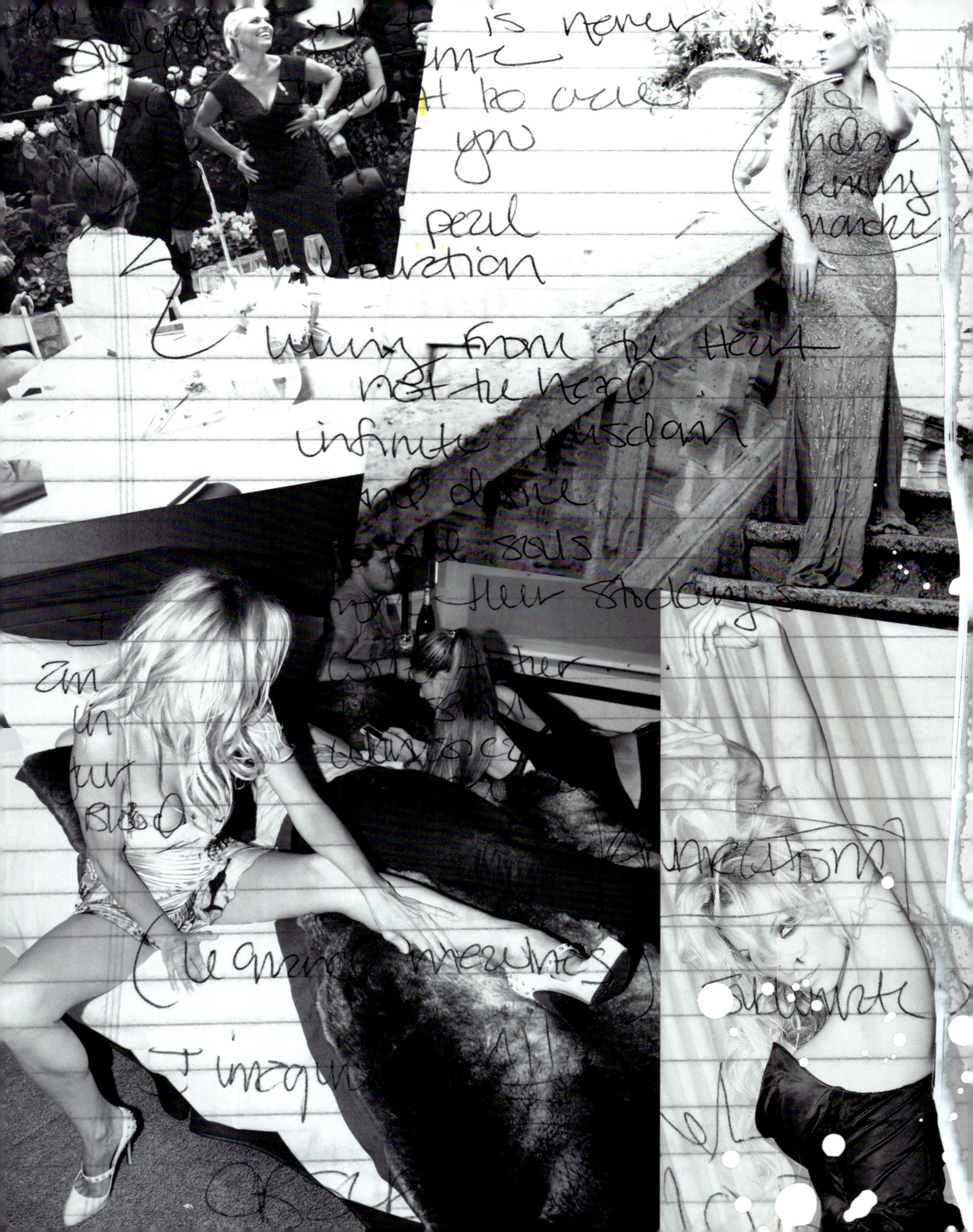

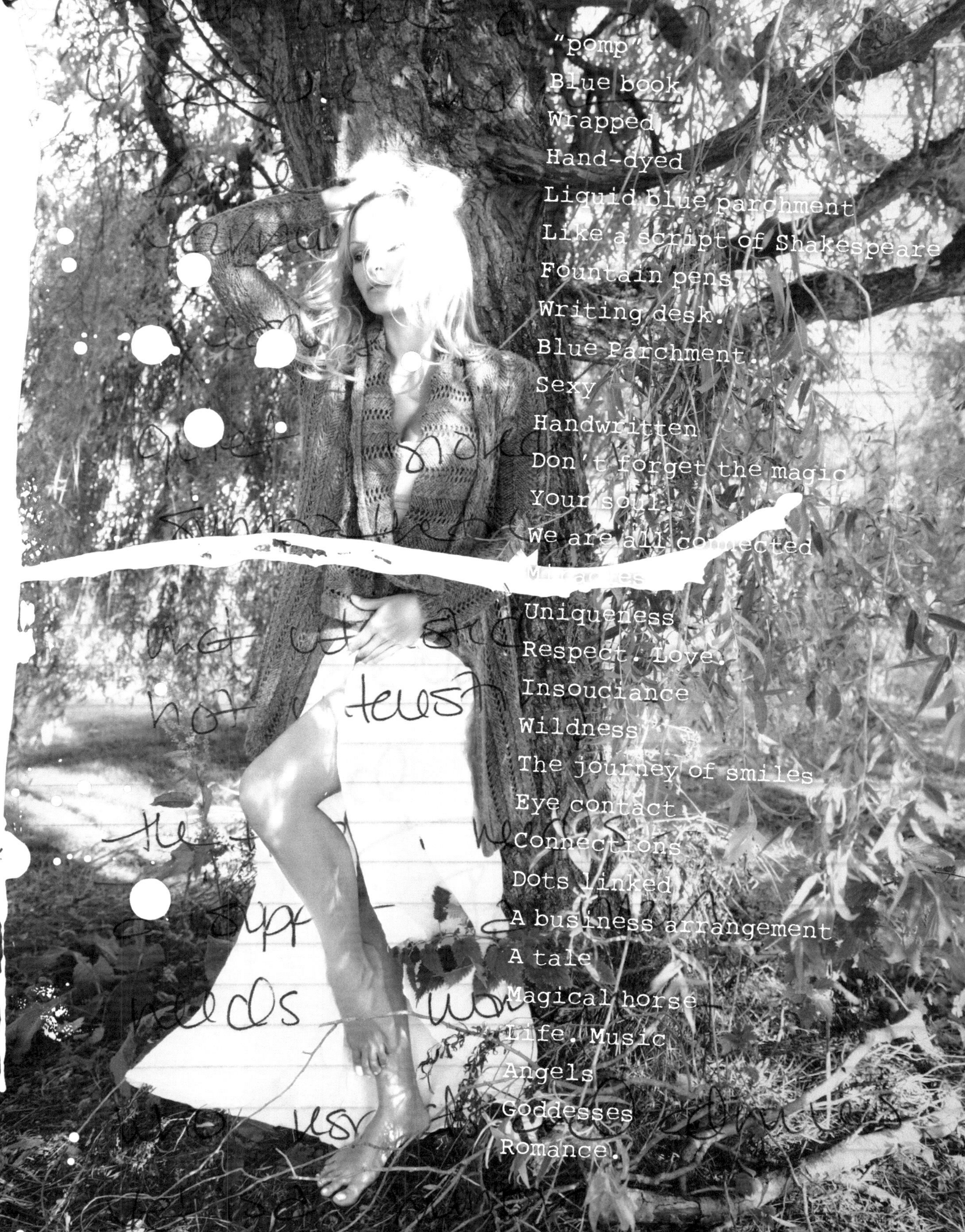
"pomp"
Blue book
Wrapped
Hand-dyed
Liquid blue parchment
Like a script of Shakespeare
Fountain pens
Writing desk.
Blue Parchment.
Sexy
Handwritten
Don't forget the magic
Your soul.
We are all connected
Uniqueness
Respect. Love
Insouciance
Wildness
The journey of smiles
Eye contact
Connections
Dots linked
A business arrangement
A tale
Magical horse
Life. Music
Angels
Goddesses
Romance.

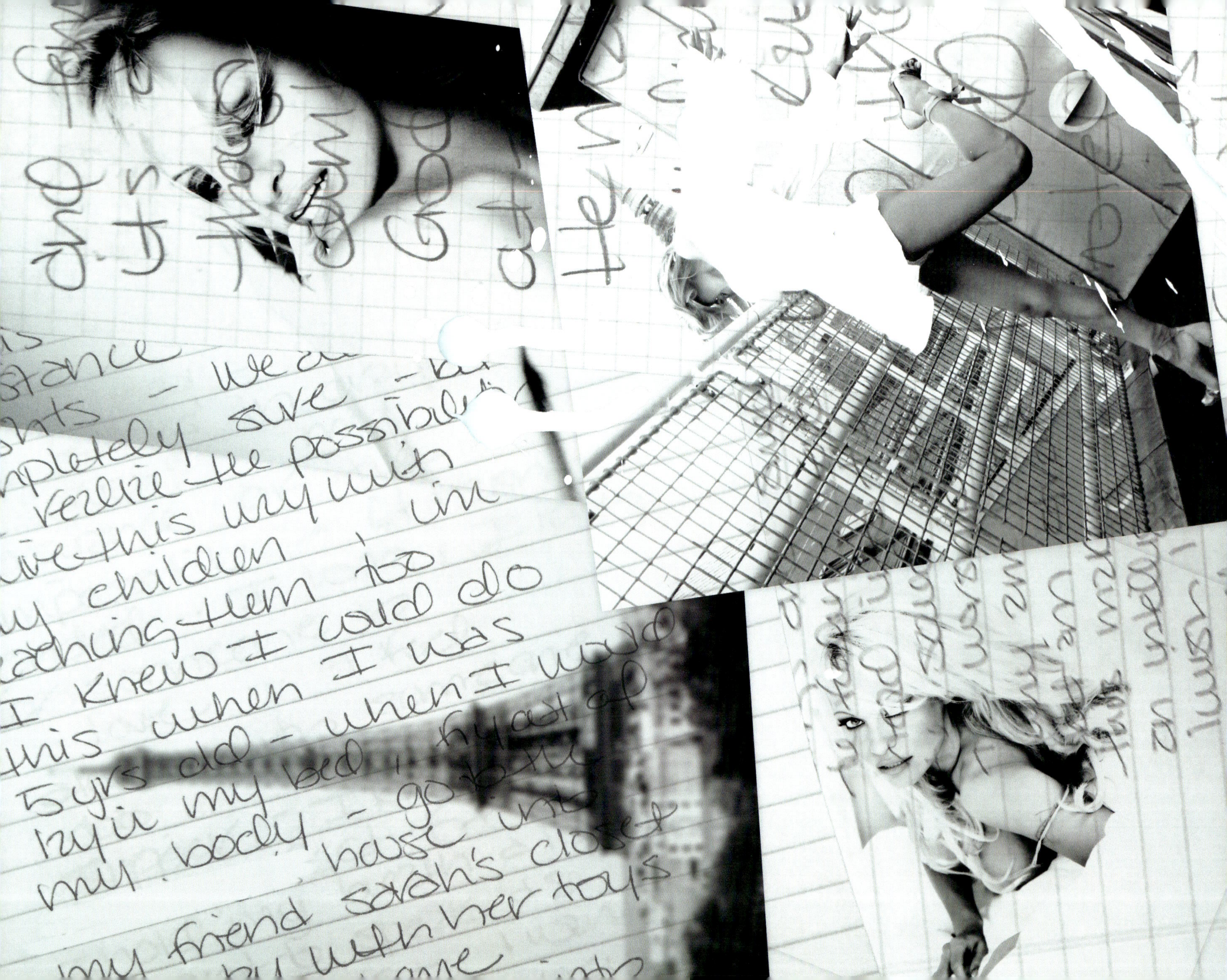

stance
ts - we a
pletely sve - k
realize the possibili
ve this way with
my children   im
aching them too
I knew I could do
this when I was
5 yrs old - when I woud
try in my bed right at
my body - go to the
house int
my friend sarah's closet
by with her toys

I havent

done it
I like my
I wont
its going
dear

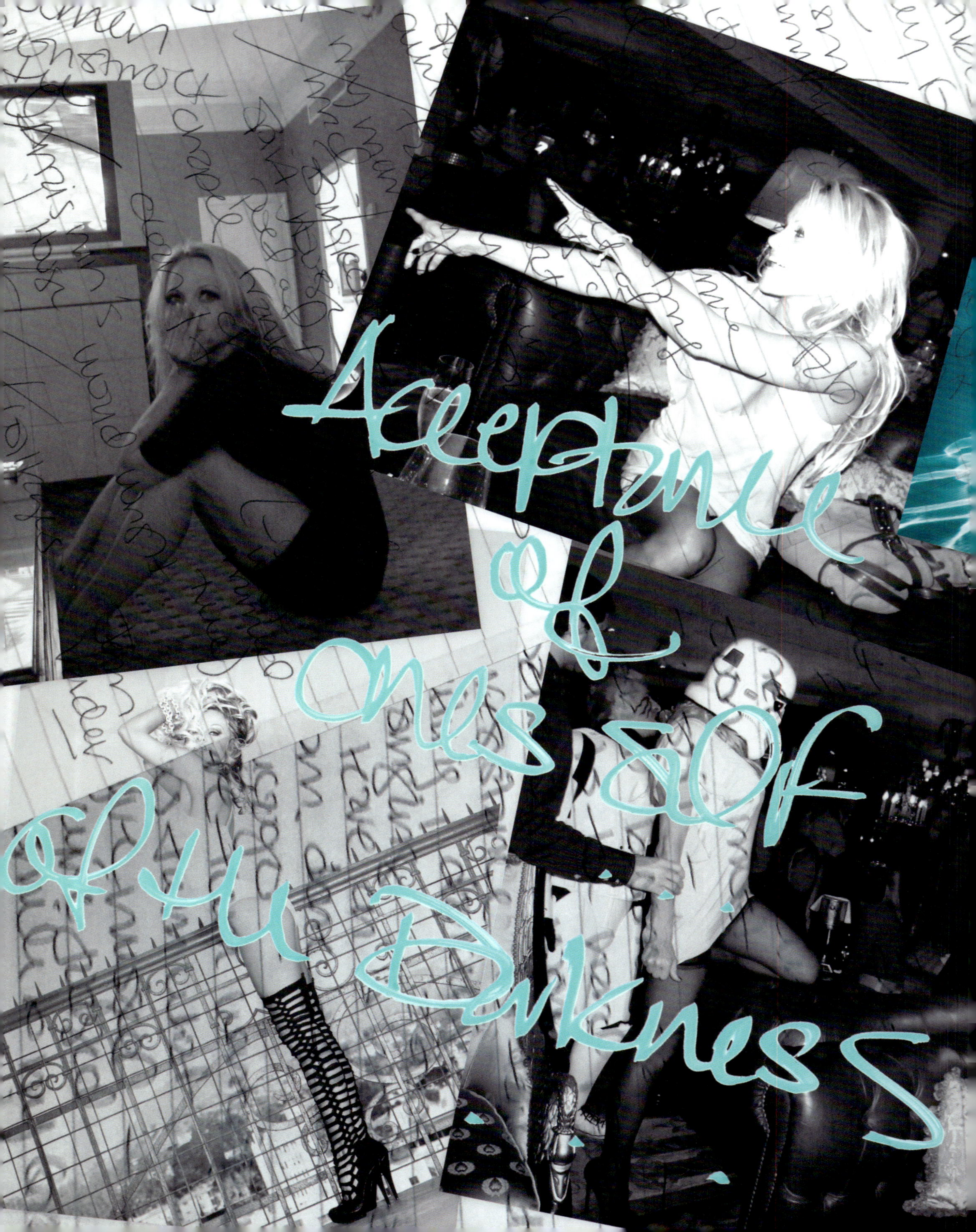
Acceptance of
ones self
of the
Darkness

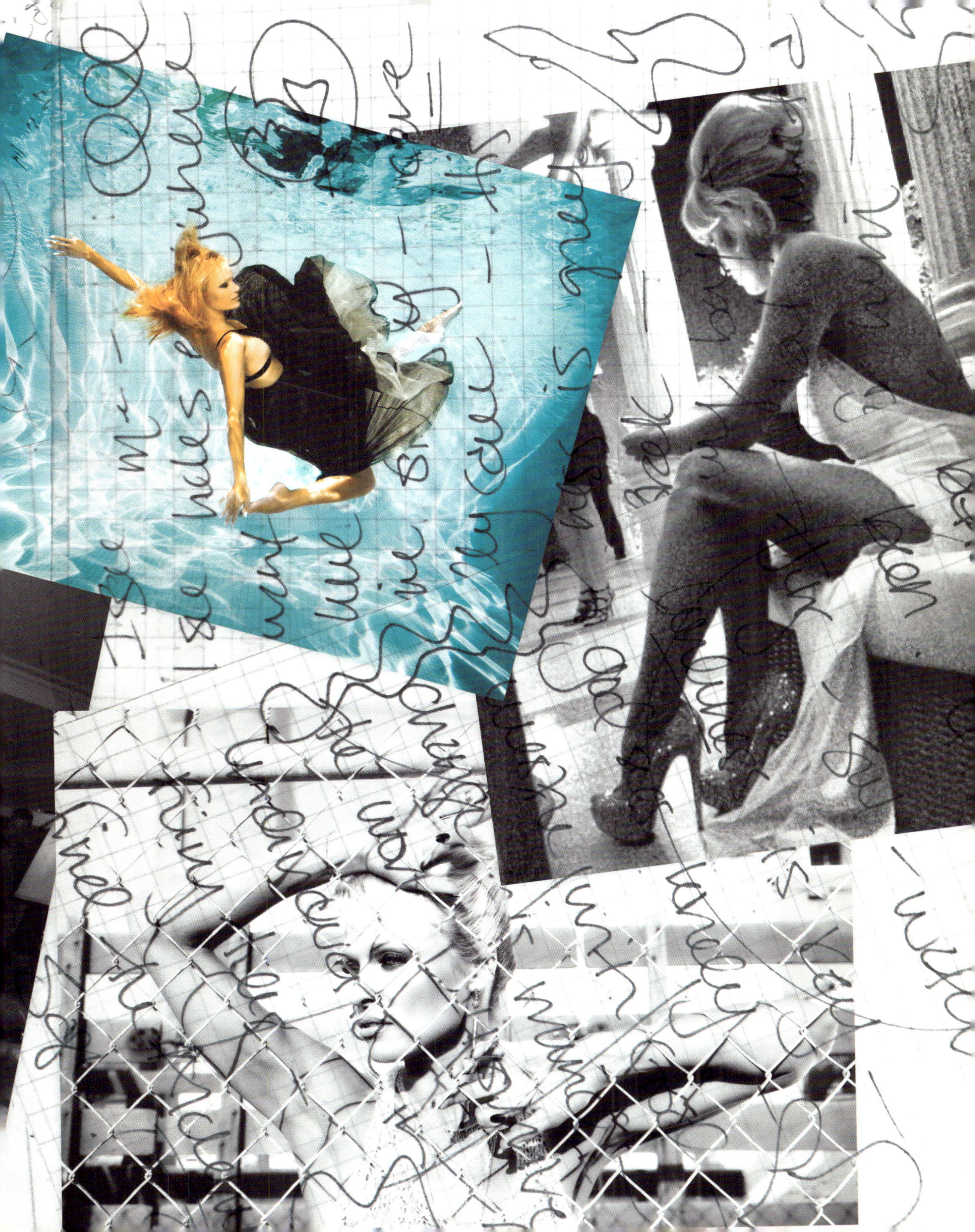

lord
[...] my family
[...] anything
[...] keep
[...] smart
don't want

and us — (just
[...] help
[...] be careful and
[...] not
[...] anymore

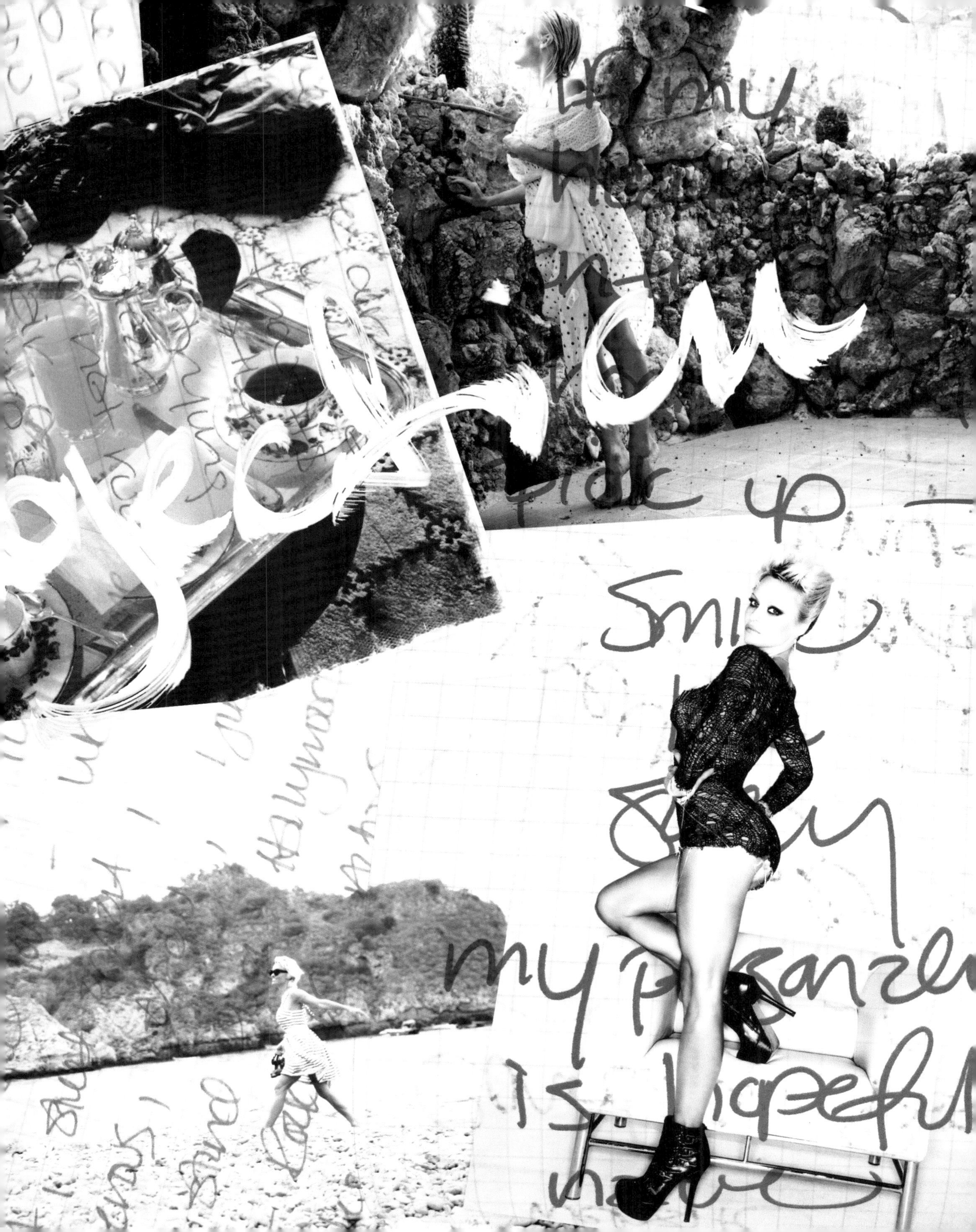

Wanton abandon
Idiosyncrasies

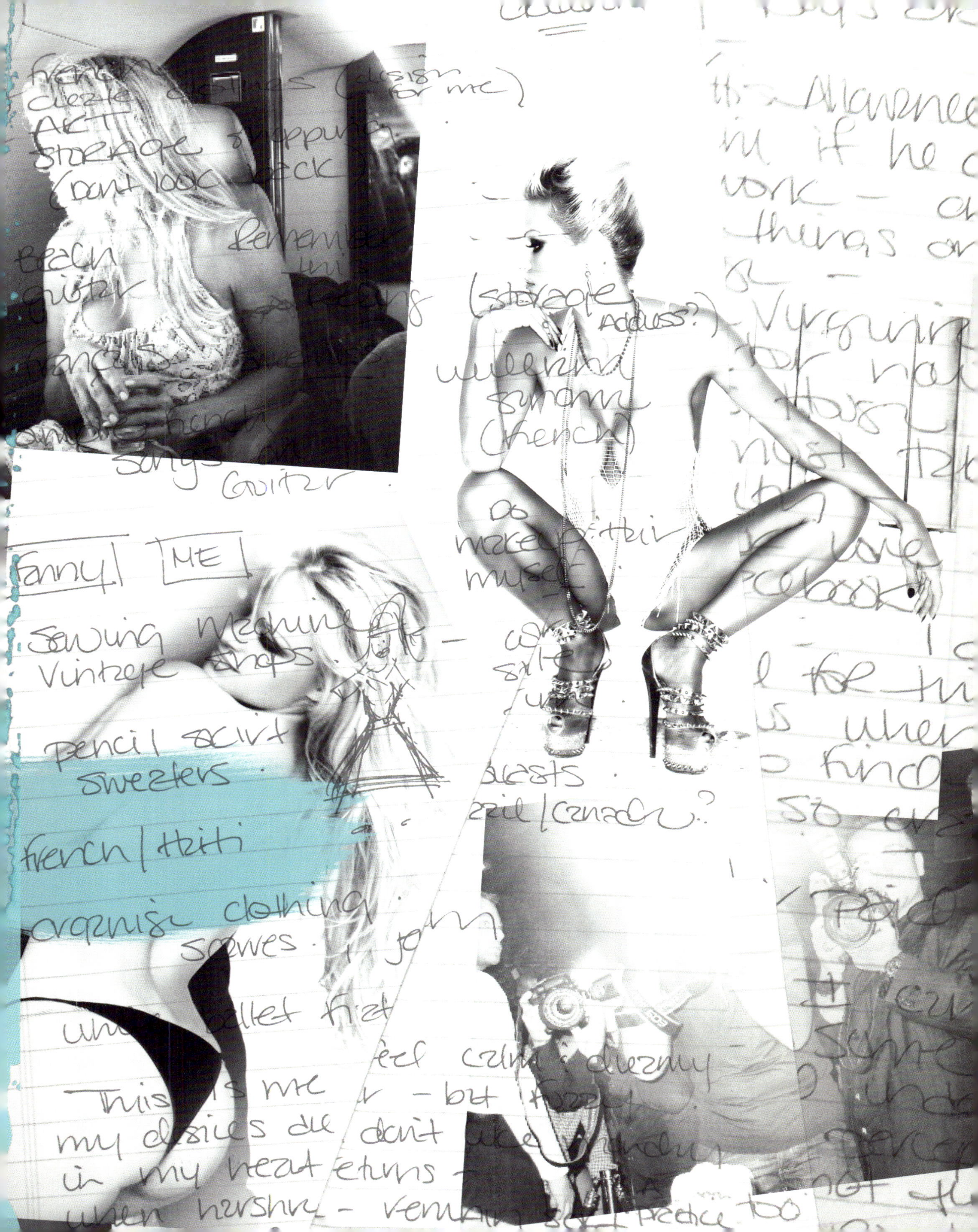

create clothes (design for me)
Art
storage shopping
(don't look back)
Beach
guitar   Remember this
songs our
Guitar

Fanny.   [ME]

Sewing Machine
Vintage shops

Pencil skirt
    sweaters

French/Haiti

organise clothing
    scarves

ballet first

This is me
my clothes do don't like
in my head etims
when

intense heart
obsessive emotional love
tortured souls —
undefined purpose — Artist
frequent —
Apparition — Apparent
chaos — love at
by Hester imprinted children
women sensitivity
numbed exposure
sensations waiting
unbound + limitless aching
life + death
less life everyone
shock + the shi
love can save
the world, compassion
...of equality
equality + passion
for supporting —
...Artists...
...long...life
...free
Paradox
true belief leads to
enlightenment

marching into Artic's
...husband
...woman
...childs graduation
...themselves
...a beautiful table
the beach
kids are excited abo-
...oldest
...weird girl
...but...athlete —
not...art)
youngest. A girl
A bit moody —
melancholy but rolling
small. Artist
performing Art school
(addictive personality)
rebelous...Whimsical
Husband. Brilliant...

Can I see you once . . .

Before . . .

Maybe a sweet rendezvous

In France?

Provence?

Walk with me . . .

A languid, lazy walk . . .

Lay in a field of lavender . . .

  ponder the sky . . . The clouds . . .

You can leave me there . . .

With the bees . . .

My greatest fear.

I'm so scared of bees.

Leave me there

To be stung . . . over and over,

A million times . . .

to death,

. . . do us part . . .

This fantasy might be over . . .

What is real?

Yesterday or tomorrow?

Day or night?

Reality or a dream . . .

You are a dream . . .

A king of kings . . .

Loves of danger

A matter of heart

A message in a bottle

A museum . . .

Heaven can wait . . .

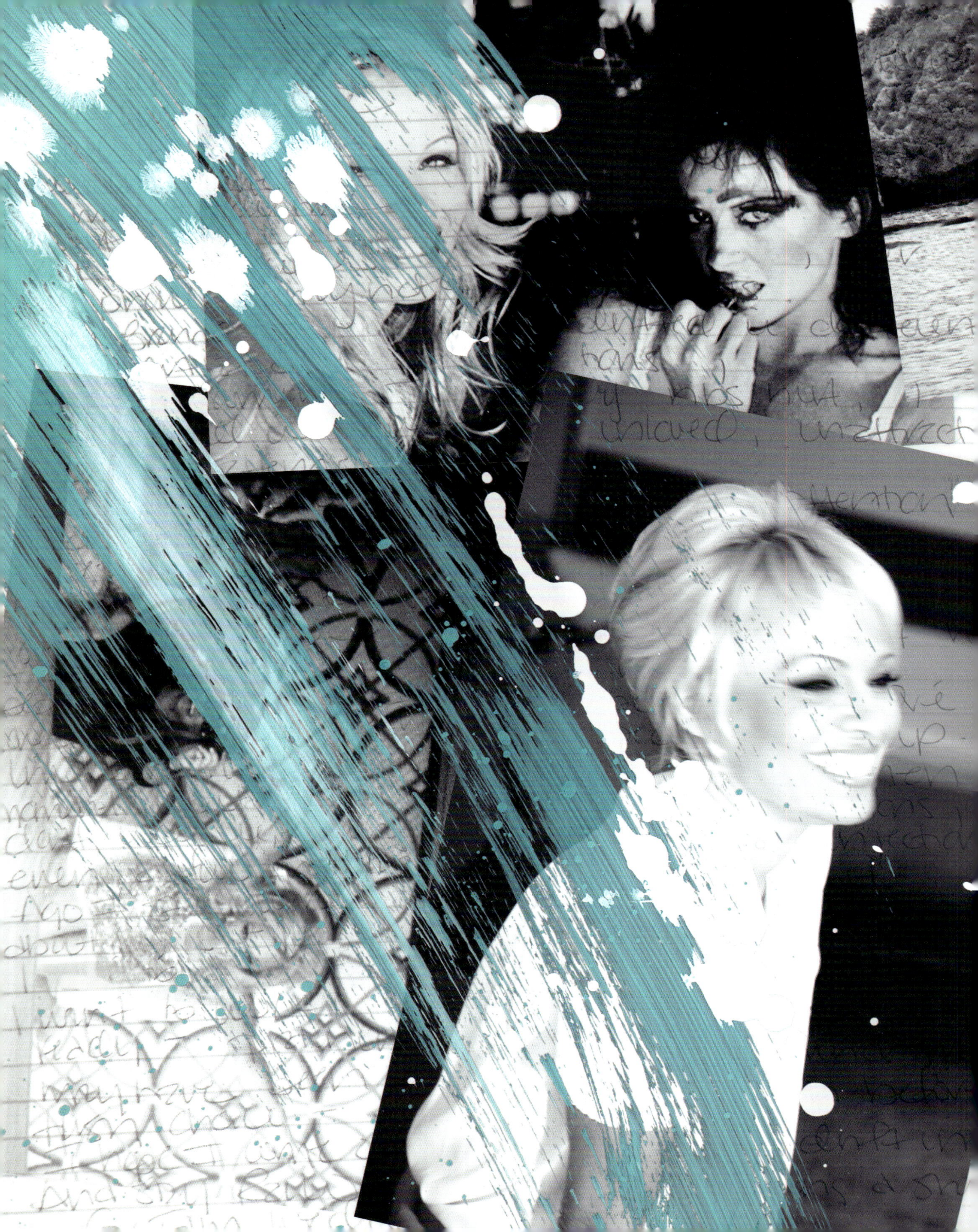

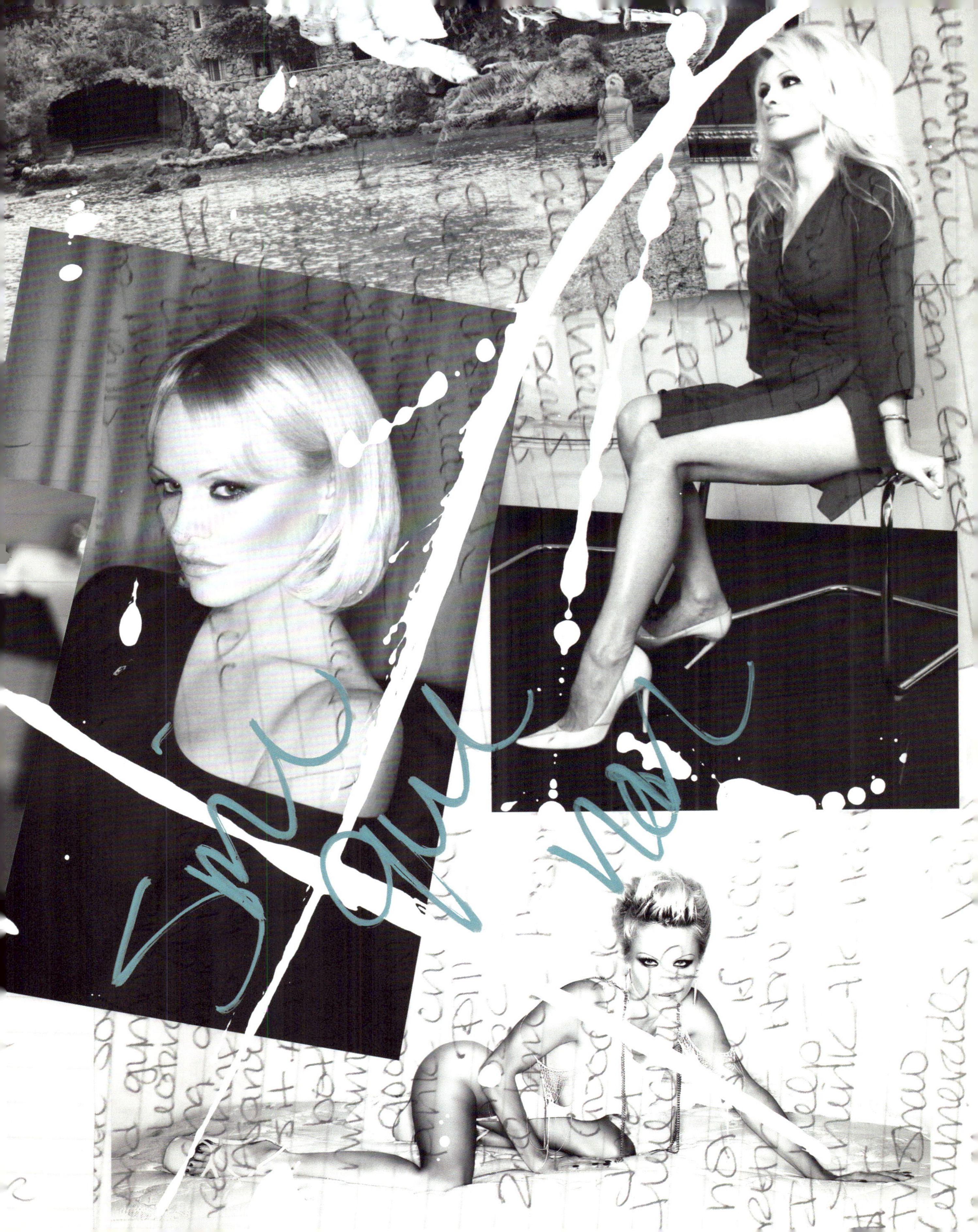

looking for

I'm deeper
searching

I see particles
trying to see
Partially

this
I need to
something

a blessing
He can't be
who needed him
be the needs to

Artists
Freedom fighters
Physical input.
Almost Androgenous
Projection
cunt Ekill demands -
love guzinels
dart

Your crazy pamela . . .
You'll see me leaving.
I'm heading home-
Walking barefoot on hot lava . . .
I turn back one last time . . . And smile . . . Before . . .
    I step into the
ocean . . . handfuls of smooth pebbles . . . drop softly at
    my sides.
I go . . . rippling . . . circles around me . . . in a
    salted halo . . .
sinking . . . slowly into the water . . . my waist, the
    lizard
queen . . . disappearing . . .
My hair floating wet behind me.
I return to my father.
It was fun baby . . .
Feel me in the flat cool rocks you skip.
Hear the melody in my voice.
The song I never sang for you resonates in your soul.
I have touched you in ways you can't forget . . .
As you have touched me . . .
In another world-you'll find me.
Dancing on a red checkered table cloth . . .
My hips swaying slowly to the memory of you inside me.
I hold myself-believing your strong arms are still
    around me.
My eyes are clothed.
A veil-not closed . . .
I'm alone . . . with tear-drenched teeth . . .
    A fantasy . . . Requited . . .
Aching ribs . . . And a liquid neck . . .
It's time to go . . . My love.
Remember me . . .

Aching
Life outside of the Sturm und Drang
of unscrupulousness
Light
Spock lover
fake Cashmere
Partners-
Darkness and poor decisions based
on instant Karma
Animal guides
Listen
Where the wind takes me.
I am not listening.
Prepare for him
Nothing is wrong
Nothing is right

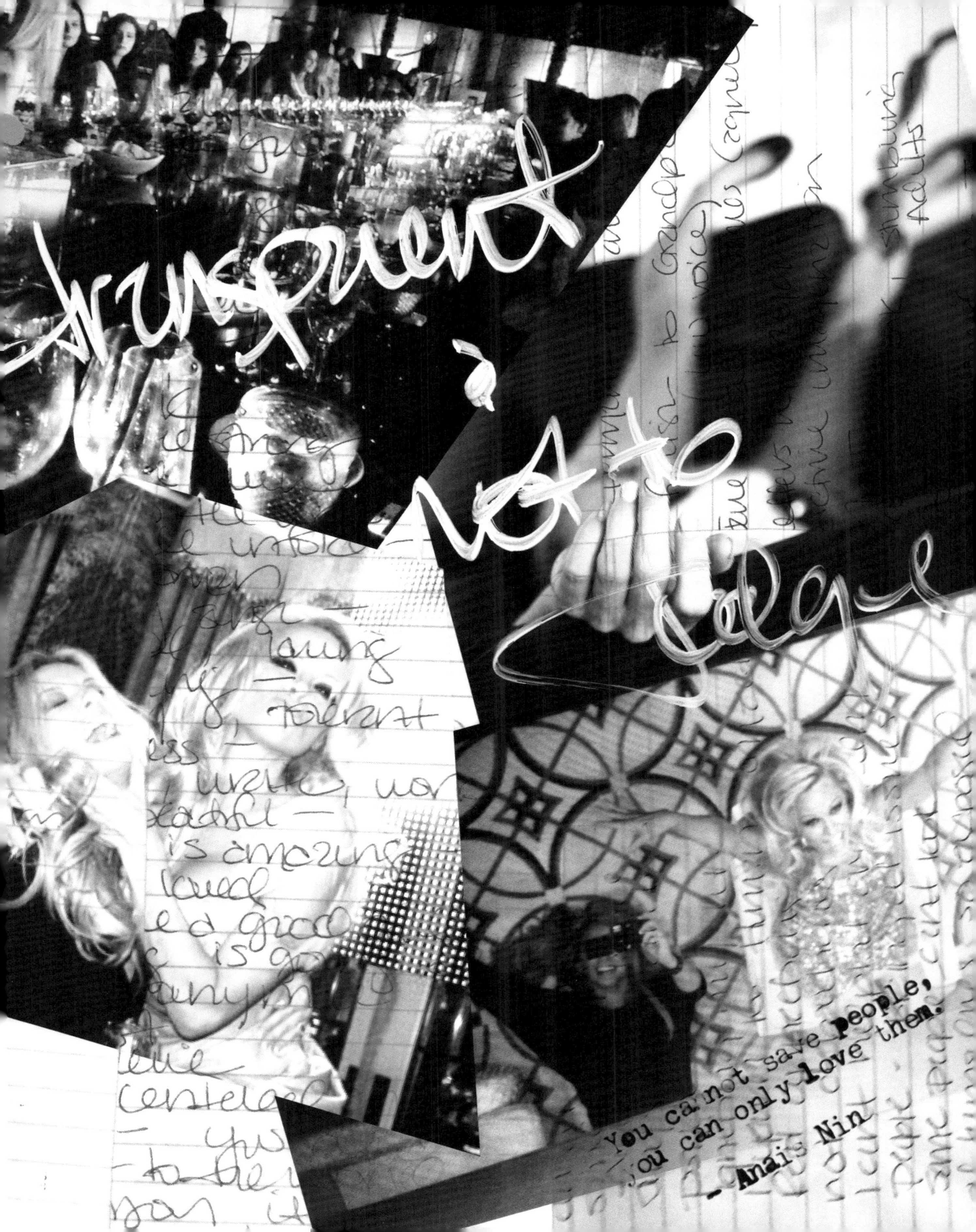

transparent
ego
...You cannot save people,
you can only love them.
— Anaïs Nin

...ship , poetry ... say
...t ownership
... rather ... better free
...woman is not
judgemental — All ... that
not nagging —
...son is not pornography
...they bring ... man
back to an erotic
...tive — woman as
...ized more than men
so we turn to each othe...
...t we can't find a creative
man —
I write to fantasize
this world is not mine
I need to embellish
it it puts —
the vulnerable, embarrassing
moments ... the truth —
addiction

Zelda Fitzgerald
wife
Caitlin Thomas

...when...
it I ... any
intimacy ... just
...? I am ... and
I have been ... bamboozled
I must feel
...t ... owned by panic
be controlled? is Hell

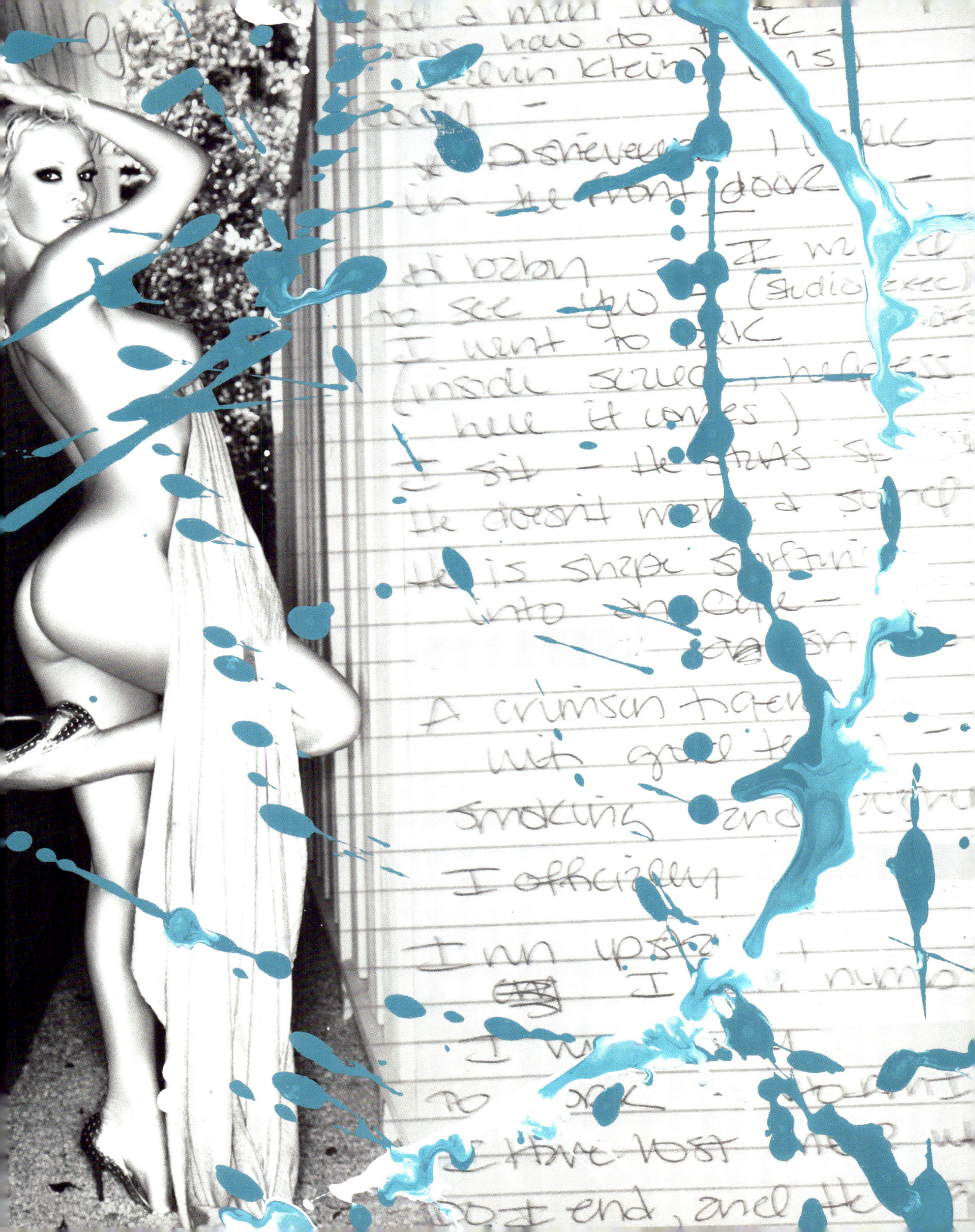

a man w[...]
was here to [...]
Kevin Klein [...]
[...]
[...] answered [...]
in the front door —

bozon — I [...]
to see you — (studio exec)
I went to ask
(inside screen, helpless
here it comes)
I sit — he gives [...]
he doesn't wear a [...]
He is shape shifting
into one eye —

A crimson tiger [...]
with great teeth
smoking and [...]

I officially

I am upset [...]
[...] I [...] numb
I went [...]
to work [...]
I have lost [...]
[...] end, and the

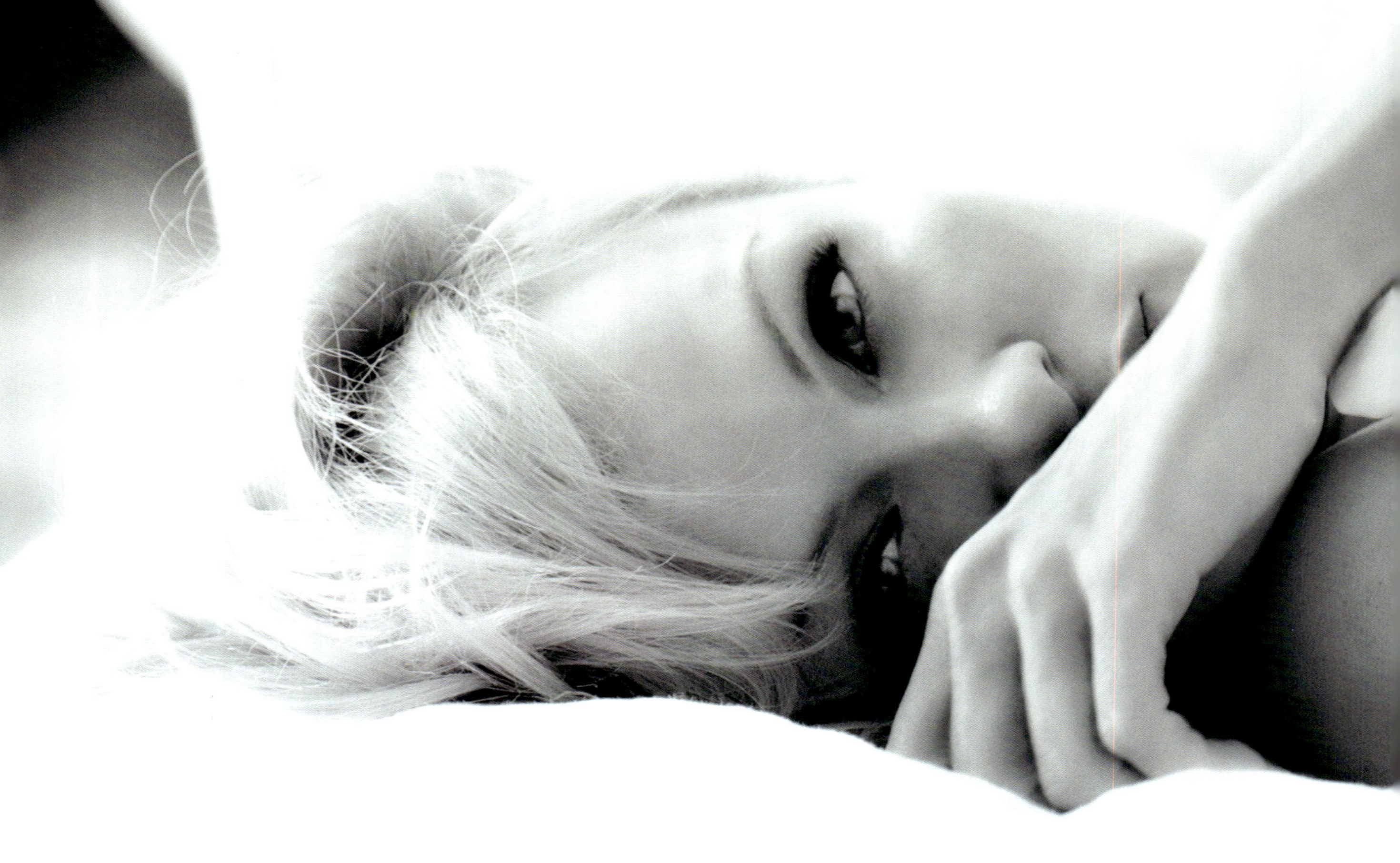

PAMELA ANDERSON is a Canadian actress, author, and activist. She founded The Pamela Anderson Foundation, which supports organizations that fight for human, animal, and environmental rights (pamelaandersonfoundation.org). She is busy writing her next book, *The Sensual Vegan* (Spring, 2016).

Small-town Canadian girl
takes her first plane ride-
to land in L.A. (on Gay Pride
Day) to shoot for Playboy . . .
(moved to L.A. in 1990)
14 American *Playboy* covers.
100s worldwide.
The "damsel in distress."
As it seemed . . .
was desired and always cared
for by powerful and talented
men . . .
Her free-spirited naivety
leads her through wild romantic
and difficult affairs.
Marrying 2 rockstars and a
professional gambler . . .
Her career-
From *Playboy* to
Baywatch, to *Barb Wire* and
Borat
Surrounded by artists.
A muse . . . an activist, a
misfit.
Two beautiful sons by
Tommy Lee.
Within a bohemian exotic life-

They have raised very grounded
and interesting sons . . .
Out of the spotlight-
shielding them from the
craziness of Hollywood,
fiercely protecting their
childhoods.
Act II of her life.
Kids are grown . . .
Full of different antics-
indie films. Raw. Natural
performances.
Characters.
More intimate and revealing
than ever.
Continuously
surprising us . . .
She is fearless and bold.
Has found the balance between
sexy and a funny self-
deprecating awareness.
Relentlessly
Compassionate . . .
Adored by men and women around
the world.

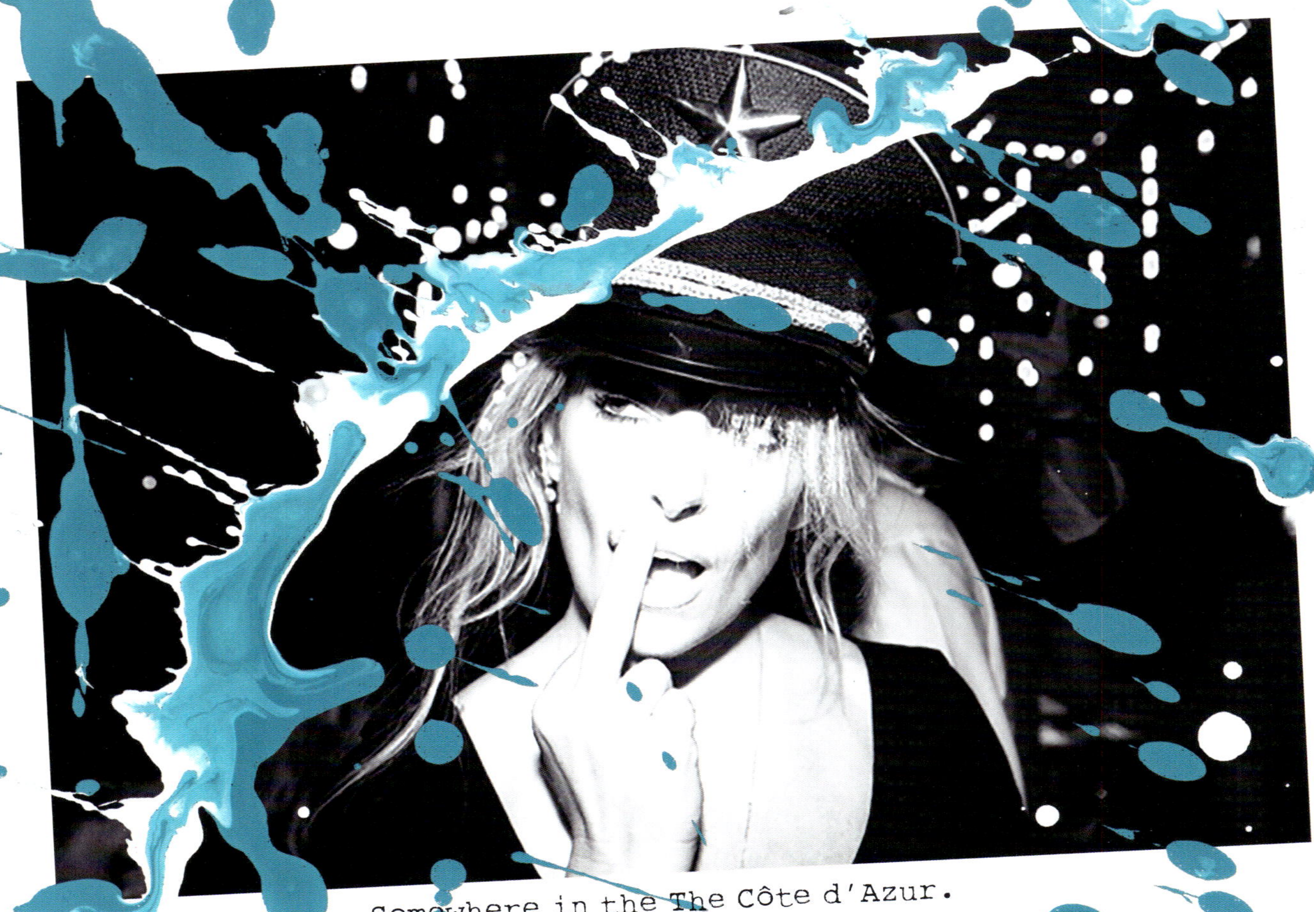

Somewhere in the The Côte d'Azur.

EMMA DUNLAVEY is a British-born photographer and artist based in Los Angeles. As a professional photographer, Emma is well known for shooting fashion, celebrities, and advertising. Her work has been published in many well respected publications worldwide. Additionally, her work and creative direction span to advertising campaigns ranging from large beverage companies to Fortune 50 companies such as Ford Motor. She has also shot campaigns for Gillette and *Architectural Digest*. Emma's other clients include Rosa Chá Brazil, BoBo (Bourgeois Boheme), Le Lis Blanc, ERRO, Pamela Couture Stockings, Woodstock Bourbon (New Zealand), Bonita de Mas, YC Jewels, PETA, Entertainment Tonight, and Endemol (Netherlands). Emma's artwork often stems from her photographic images. She works with beautiful resins and mixed media and uses a process of layering different imagery. She often incorporates 3-D objects into her pieces that give both elevated visual and tactile elements to her work.

Emma's true passion is shooting the strength and beauty of women-capturing the "real moment" and glimpsing through the intimate window between photographer and subject. Learn more about her work at emmadunlavey.com.

ARTIST'S STATEMENT: I look back at pictures of me and Pamela from twenty years ago—time really does fly when you're having fun! Over the years, we have shared our most intimate feelings and life events, which have made our bond incredibly close; in a sense, we have grown up together. I love Pamela for exactly who and what she is; she is like a sister to me. I am a huge admirer of her beauty, power, and vulnerability. Her heart is as big as the ocean. But she is the iron fist in a silk glove!

It's been an incredible journey over the years. I've travelled all over the world with Pamela. I have seen amazing places, had incredible experiences, and have met so many inspirational people.

And all along I have shot photos *behind* the behind-the-scenes of Pamela—truly spontaneous, unplanned, ninja-style shooting. How exciting to share these intimate, wild, funny images with the world in *Raw*. What an incredible life it is!

I have branched into art, which seemed a natural progression from photography. My big art pieces generally stem from my photographs. It's all a creative journey of expression. I visualize pieces of art involving mixed media, resin, 3-D objects—a synergy of words, photography, and paint, which I see in my head already complete... and layer by layer they are realized and formed. When I am lost for words I communicate through the visual. Like speaking in silence to be heard through the eyes. Just as when I am shooting pictures, I am completely alive and connected when I'm creating my art. It's very hands-on and tactile—there is energy flowing through everything, and perhaps this is the connection I feel... whatever it is...it is addictive.

When I am home by the beach, surrounded by my loving family, I often still pinch myself and wonder if this is really my life. A little girl from a tiny village in the English countryside, I do have a very strong belief in visualization and that anything is possible, but still...just proves that if you believe, work hard, and trust in the universe...dreams really do come true!

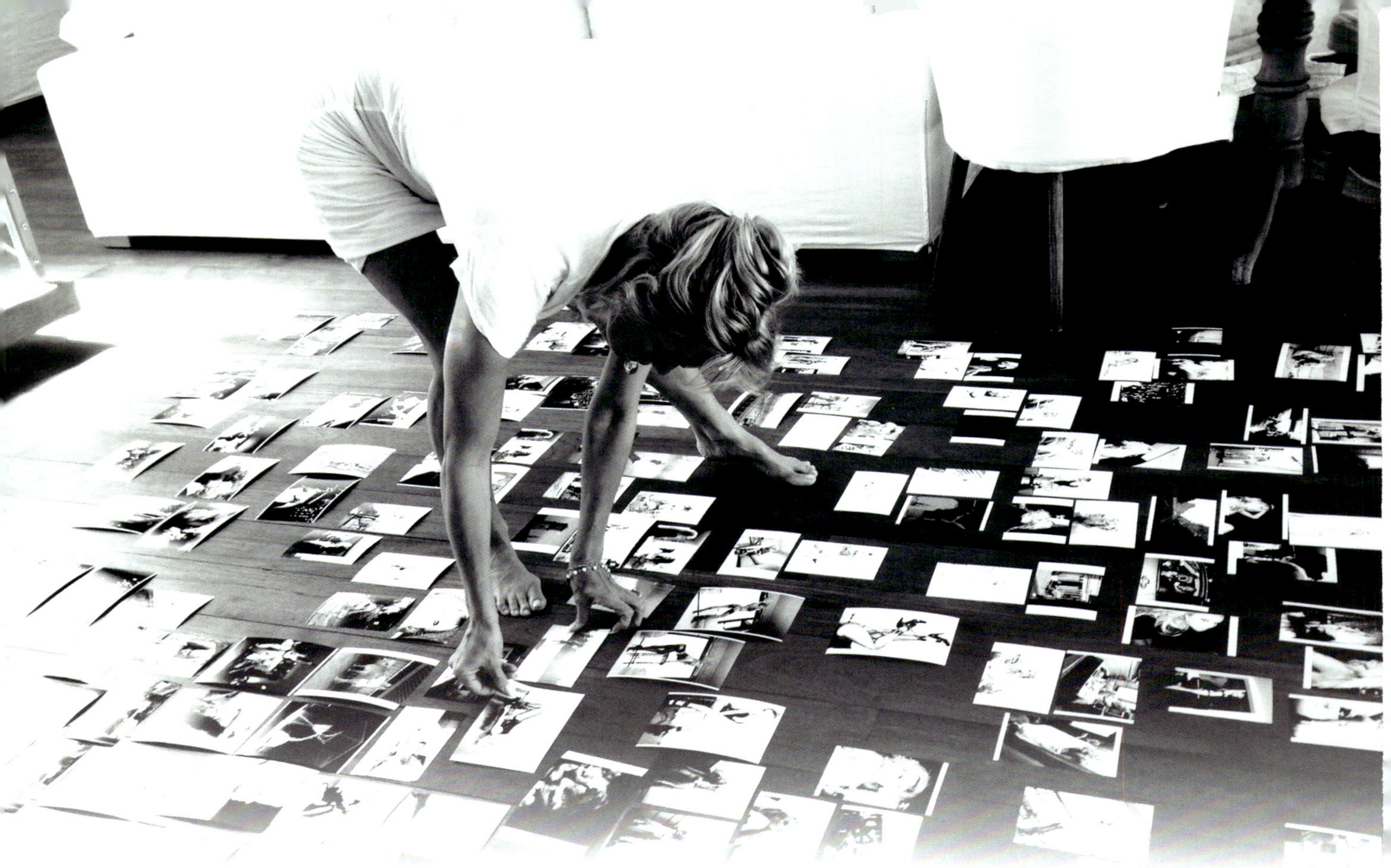

BenBella Books, Inc.
10300 N. Central Expressway
Suite #530
Dallas, TX 75231
www.benbellabooks.com

Send feedback to
feedback@benbellabooks.com

Printed and bound in the U.S.A.
10 9 8 7 6 5 4 3 2 1

Project Manager:
Sarah Dombrowsky
Production Manager:
Monica Lowry
Design and Typesetting:
Aaron Edmiston
Production Support:
Jessika Rieck
Cover design and layout:
Sarah Dombrowsky

Library of Congress data available upon request.

Photographs copyright
© Emma Dunlavey
www.emmadunlavey.com

Select images © Emma Dunlavey/
Courtesy of Getty Images

Distributed by Perseus Distribution
www.perseusdistribution.com

To place orders through Perseus Distribution:
Tel: (800) 343-4499
Fax: (800) 351-5073
E-mail:
orderentry@perseusbooks.com